One Day At a Time

Words Of Wisdom To Live By and Learn From

Written By

Larissa T. McCormick, Ph. D.

To Tell HerStory LLC
Indianapolis, IN

ToTellHerStoryLLC@yahoo.com

This book is a work of nonfiction. However, the quotations, explanations, interpretations, perspectives, and prompts (the collective of creative expressions) do not provide specific advice and are to be taken as suggestions and/or offerings.

Copyright © 2021 by Larissa T. McCormick, Ph.D.

All rights reserved, including the right to reproduce this book or portions thereof in any form whatsoever.

Dedication

I offer this book of quotations (also called "quotables") to students, educators, youth, adults, mentees, mentors, optimists, pessimists, inspirers, change agents, and any individual who feels that it is their mission (or choice) in life to encourage others to exist, act, and think most favorably with/about others, life, humanity, society, and themselves as it applies to their aspirations, shortcomings, and day-to-day experiences, whether of great or small significance.

I give this book to my loving Mother. You have always believed in me, supported me, and encouraged me to share my God-given talents and gifts with the world. It is because of your daily inspiration and positivity into the lives of your children and grandchild that this book exists Mommy. (I would also like to thank you for lending your wisdom and insight (as well as eyes) to the fruition of this book.

Preface

The inspiration for this book came from my admiration for (my) students, the field of education, the vocation of educators, and my belief that positive and uplifting words are vital for human (student) development and growth—spiritual, mental, emotional, and social. In my classroom, room 207, I have more than 300 quotations from distinguished, yet to be known, and anonymous individuals as well as my own (noted within parentheses in this book) displayed on walls, boards, windows, ledges, desks, tables, cabinets, countertops, bookshelves, and the door for students and any other visitors to gain insight from, be stimulated by, and view alternative words of positivity, encouragement, uplift, and support.

It is my sincerest belief that everyone needs someone to instill positive thoughts into their mind (being) daily. Everyone needs to have their soul inspired to be better people, to do better for humanity and the world, and to live better for others and themself. Everyone needs opportunities to develop their endowed potential despite their past or present circumstances, race or ethnicity, and age or gender. Everyone does not have access to such opportunities in their immediate (and distant) environment—home, school, community, and society. Consequently, this book of quotations is necessary and can fill that void or further that potential.

On March 13, 2020, life as most people knew it was interrupted, put on-hold, and forever changed. All systems within society underwent modification to some degree. People became uncertain, afraid, and more or less pessimistic or optimistic. Interpersonal communication, interaction, and exchange between human beings across the globe became according to many individuals altered, fragmented, and nonexistent. In light of this book, schools, the educational system, and the manner by which educational institutions did business was radically uprooted "overnight." Students possibly more than educators (and parent/guardians) were forced into a state of perpetual flux. Despite the efforts of many, some semblance of how things once were quickly became a too often recalled memory. Since then, time has passed. People have changed, whether for the better or worse. Society has learned to adapt to the "new normal." (A phrase that has become a part of the post {onset of the} COVID-19 pandemic lexicon.) Systems have returned to functioning as close if not as they once operated. Nevertheless, one constant remained—the need for kindness in one's daily existence.

Being kind to another human being despite one's feelings and beliefs is an essential variable in the equation of love. Kindness shown equates kindness received. Encouragement given equates encouragement received. Positivity shared equates positivity received. Simply stated in 1965, "what the world needs now is love" (Hal David and Burt Bacharach). *One Day At a Time: Words Of Wisdom To Live By and Learn From* is a great way to begin or continue loving.

Day 1

One day at a time.

Each day of life you are given an opportunity to do, to be, to learn, to live, to love, to make a difference, and to start a new. It is true that each day offers opportunities and experiences that can be viewed as positive, as negative, or as neutral. Sometimes, it seems as if those opportunities are out of your control. Even if those opportunities or experiences appear too difficult, to be in the hands of another, or even insurmountable, you can be the orchestrator of your outcome, a victor, and attain the level of success that you desire. First, you must take each day as they come, one day at a time. No one knows everything that tomorrow will bring. However, each day, focus on and make the most of every opportunity and experience because your reaction has the power to impact not only that day but the days to come in life.

Writing/Journal/Action/Discussion/Reflection Prompt:

How will you moving forward approach life one day at a time?

Day 2

Follow your own way.

Have you ever been given a choice between following someone and following your own sense of direction? Deep within, you sense the urging of going in your own direction. Possibly, it is easier to follow the direction and guidance of another, even if you do not have 100% confidence in the guidance of that individual. It is alright to take the lead, especially when you have weighed the alternative. Follow your own way; in doing so, the path you take will most likely lead you to the destination that you seek.

Writing/Journal/Action/Discussion/Reflection Prompt:

Discuss a time in your life when you chose to follow your own way even if someone else offered to assist you in the process. Do you feel that you made the best decision for yourself?

Day 3

Hope is the only thing stronger than fear.

Fear is often described as false evidence appearing real. Fear has the power to control, to consume, and to overtake every aspect of existence. It is impossible for fear to turn reality into the unimaginable. When this happens, fear guides you in the wrong direction and forces you to doubt what is known as well is what is unknown. You can overcome your fear by focusing your energy on what you want to happen—expectations. When you allow expectations to guide you, fear begins to loosen its grip as well as its power. Before you realize it, you are motivated by positive possibilities and expectations often described as hope.

Writing/Journal/Action/Discussion/Reflection Prompt:

What is your greatest fear? In what ways can you reimagine that fear so that it becomes hope?

Day 4

Dream it... Wish it... Do it...

Have you ever wanted something to happen in life that you could not imagine was possible to happen, especially for you? You are not alone! Every day someone somewhere imagines a reality for themself that they and/or others could never foresee possible. Understand that you are allowed to believe in the impossible and the realm of the unthinkable; this is often called dreaming. When you dream, you are believing that something that is not presently as you wish it will by some happening become that something that you desire. For many things to be as you want them to be in life, you must take action. Action very often leads to desired results. You must do your part in causing to happen what you want to happen in life each day. Remember, most things that happen in life that you truly want to happen are the result of dreaming, wishing, and doing.

Writing/Journal/Action/Discussion/Reflection Prompt:

What is something that you want to happen in your life? Consider within the span of the next month, the next six months, the next year, and beyond in your life. Create a plan. Put action to that plan. See the unfolding results, and watch your dreams become your reality.

Day 5

"Be the change you want to see in the world."
Mahatma Gandhi

You have the ability to make and be the difference in another person's life, whether for a short-term or a long-term and have a minor or major impact. Throughout your life, without doubt, you have seen many instances in our world and close to home where injustice, inequality, and indifference have been on display. You have seen these displays whether directly or indirectly acted upon people, places, things, and ideas/concepts. Possibly, these displays stirred within you anger, mistrust, fear, and sorrow. In turn, your reaction motivated you to action or at least inspired you to want to take some form of action in opposition to what you had witnessed in the world. This is what Mahatma Ghandi meant when he said, "Be the change…."

Writing/Journal/Action/Discussion/Reflection Prompt:

How can you honor the request of Ghandi to the members of the global society, now and in the future?

Day 6

Open your heart to new adventures.

The experiences that you have in life can negatively impact you. In fact, these experiences can make you bitter, angry, and close-off to things, people, and ideas that could otherwise be exciting, appealing, and inviting to you. Understand that everyone experiences such happenings, but the difference lies in how you respond to those experiences. The next time that you encounter situations that have the potential to negatively change your outlook, commit to permitting the opposite to occur in your perception. Open your heart to a different outcome. You will be amazed at not only where the experience leads you but also at what new adventures await you. Adventure that you might have missed because of those negative impacts.

Writing/Journal/Action/Discussion/Reflection Prompt:

Think about a time in your life when you had an experience that negatively impacted you. Now, think about that same experience from the perspective of allowing a positive outcome. How would your life be different from the way that it is today? What adventure did you completely miss or deter by permitting the negative to take precedence rather than the positive?

Day 7

The best way to predict the future is to create it.

Very often in life, you hope for things that are imaginable, but you find yourself stopping short of stepping in the direction that will lead you towards your desire. Why do you do this? You do this simply because you do not want to fall short of reaching your goal. You do not want to disappoint someone or even yourself. Most importantly, you neither want to be viewed as "failing" nor even labeled a "failure." You would rather not try than not succeed. The next time that you are inclined to step out in a new direction towards the future that you want in life, remember, it begins by taking the first step, and following that step by another. When you look ahead, what was once in the unforeseen distance is now only a few more steps ahead of you. You are creating your future.

Writing/Journal/Action/Discussion/Reflection Prompt:

Identify something that you want to happen in your future, whether near or distant with respect to time. Now, draft a plan as to how you can make your future hope a personal reality. Be realistic and consider the known factors that might get in your way. When you finish with the draft, put it into action and walk or run into your future.

Day 8

Set your goals high and do not stop until you get there. Believe you can and you are halfway there.

When you begin something new in life, it is all right to set what might seem like an "unrealistic" goal, especially to others. However, you know better than anyone else what lies within you, even if it is only at the stage of a seedling. You have the power to achieve what you set your mind to do in life. It will not always be easy, and the answer will not always be obvious. Remember, determination is the key. If you miss the mark, keep trying until you reach it, whatever it is that you want in life. Try to erase self-doubt, and tune-out the doubt offered by others that is not reasonable or coming from a place of love. Trust yourself. Believe in yourself. Before you know it, you have accomplished that goal and are onto accomplishing the next goal.

Writing/Journal/Action/Discussion/Reflection Prompt:

Name a goal for yourself that appears to be unrealistic to others or even yourself. Write three action steps that you need to take to begin working towards that goal. Once you accomplish those steps, write three more. Repeat. Soon, you will have achieved what you and possibly others thought could not be done.

Day 9

Keep moving forward.

The opposite of forward is backward. Not too many people walk in the reverse direction through life. Of course, there are times in life when you might want to reverse time or have a second chance at something or with someone. Even during those times, do you really want to erase everything that came before that moment? Pause and reflect. Consider what if anything could have been done differently, and apply it to the next time or a similar situation that arises in your life. Chances are that it will help you move forward rather than remaining stuck in the moment for longer than the needed amount of time. Certainly, it is the most preferred option and helps you make a better-informed decision as you move in a forward rather than backward direction.

Writing/Journal/Action/Discussion/Reflection Prompt:

Write about a decision that you made in life that you would have liked to have had the opportunity to make/do again. Did that decision hold you back, propel you forward, or cause you to revert to former behaviors or thinking? In your response, consider one thing that could have turned the negative outcome into a positive outcome, or the positive outcome into a negative outcome. Decide how you will respond moving forward.

Day 10

Radiate positivity.

When you radiate, you release and give off energy that either attracts or repels. Is it not better when you send into the universe positive vibes? Remember, people invite what they give out, even unintentionally. Rarely is anyone at their best 100% of the time; there might be two or three exceptions in history! This is because we are human, and we respond to what happens to us and through us. The next time that you are in a mood, hold an opinion, react to someone or something else in a manner that you think might affect others in a negative way, and try to express encouragement rather than discouragement.

Writing/Journal/Action/Discussion/Reflection Prompt:

How can you respond to or interact more positively with those who you agree and disagree with in the future? Be specific and include both how and why you usually respond to those individuals.

Day 11

Be a kind human.

Inhabitants of the world represent all types of people, and there exist all types of descriptors to label, classify, and define the people. Male, female (gender); Black, White (race); liberal, conservative (political affiliation); Christian and non-Christian (religion); Eastern, Western (location by Earth's hemisphere); and hundreds more descriptors. Consequently, people often use these descriptors as a rationale for treating others unjustly, unequally, and differently than they do other people, specifically those with whom they relate. This often leads to actions, words, and practices that are unkind. Regardless of the descriptors that you choose to use, no one can argue the one descriptor that unites us—human. If you always remember that your humanity unites rather than divides you from another human being, you are inclined to practice kindness rather than its converse.

Writing/Journal/Action/Discussion/Reflection Prompt:

What is the harm in being kind even when others are not kind to you? For five minutes, write as much as you can in response to this question. Review your response, and implement strategies in your life where you can intentionally practice kindness.

Day 12

Have a beautiful day.

You deserve it. Everyone deserves it. It is has been said, "Life will throw you curve balls." This means that you will have those "unexpected" and "out-of-your-control" occurrences in life. In those times, meet the experiences head-on and know that you will overcome your challenges. Remember, whatever, positive or negative, comes to you in your lifetime does not disqualify you from enjoying and relishing in the fact that you have been given another day of life. That very fact is beauty to the tenth degree.

Writing/Journal/Action/Discussion/Reflection Prompt:

Write about a time that you chose to see your day as the opposite of beautiful. Next, write about how that day could have changed if you had viewed it as beautiful. Moving forward, try to see the beauty in each day.

Day 13

Life is what you make it.

This statement aligns with the thought of "the glass as half full or half empty." You always have the choice to view your life—situations, experiences, and events—from an optimistic or a pessimistic perspective. It is very certain that your perspective will change based upon the circumstances. However, do not allow the perspective of others or one event, situation, or experience to affect future events, situations, or experiences. Life is about perspective and is the result of which viewpoint you will permit to have more influence over the other.

Writing/Journal/Action/Discussion/Reflection Prompt:

A frown viewed from the opposite perspective is a smile. Consider that statement and provide your perspective of it. Do you agree or disagree with the statement? Why or why not?

Day 14

Inhale courage; exhale fear.

Courage and fear are the antithesis of each other. When one is present, the other is absent. When one is dominant, the other is subordinate. When one is strong, the other is weak. It is a guarantee that you will feel and demonstrate either one of these emotions throughout your lifetime, and that is all right. You should never consider yourself to be anything other than "human" when either one of these emotions are present in your life. Remember, no one person is always courageous, and no one person should always be fearful. In times of fear, courage can take over and vice versa. Learn ways to find a balance between both emotions. Just breathe!

Writing/Journal/Action/Discussion/Reflection Prompt:

Identify a time when you were courageous or fearful. How could you have demonstrated the opposite emotion in that situation?

Day 15

My brain has too many tabs open.

Your brain is operating 24-hours each day. There might be times when you would like to stop or pause all the processes of your brain but you cannot. Sometimes, you have so many tasks to complete or items to check-off your "To Do" list that your thoughts can appear or become overwhelming. Actually, you are not alone. Others feel the same way. During these times, you might envision your mind as a computer with too many browser tabs open, which can result in delays in and overload of processing information; this too happens to your brain in ways. In such instances, try to use some type of relaxation technique, prayer, or mediation. Take time to focus on one task or item at a time. Ultimately, you will not only complete things with more clarity, but also you will alleviate some of the potential stress.

Writing/Journal/Action/Discussion/Reflection Prompt:

What have you done in the past to handle mental stress? Find a new approach to handling mental stress and apply it in a future situation.

Day 16

Thinking of a master plan.

You are not alone if you have dreamt of another way to do something, imagine yourself, or make a positive difference in someone's life or society. It is possible that you even thought of a way that seemed impossible or out-of-reach. Do not give-up or give-in to those thoughts. Realize that some endeavors require more thought, energy, time, and resources than other endeavors. Each of these factors are essentials in devising a "master plan." A master plan is a strategy that influences and impacts the lives of people not just one person, decades and not just one year, and changes the way in which systems and not just one system promote sustainable positive change. Next time that you experience that impossible thought, do not be so quick to dismiss it. Rather, create a master plan to accomplish your thought.

Writing/Journal/Action/Discussion/Reflection Prompt:

What is your master plan? In what ways have, you thought your plan to be unattainable. What is one immediate step that you can take to begin working towards accomplishing your plan? Next, execute the first step and continue moving forward.

Day 17

Make it happen!

Can another person make happen for you what you want to happen without you being a part of the process? Rarely does that happen in life, if truly ever it happens. You are on this Earth for a certain purpose. With that in mind, you are the needed variable in what happens in your life. Life should not be a passive experience, and it was not fashioned in that way either. Rather, life is an active experience. Do not allow others to send you down the path that is not for you to travel. If you want something, you must make it happen. Take part in the process and enjoy the reward(s).

Writing/Journal/Action/Discussion/Reflection Prompt:

What is something that you want to happen in the next year? Detail how you will take an active role in making that situation happen for you.

Day 18

(Just a female/male boss building his/her empire.)

Girl power! Boy Power! These are real! You possess it! Every day you have the opportunity to create, unleash, and experience the power that radiates from females and males. Too often in society, the power that an individual possesses is diminished and overlooked in order to accommodate the power of the collective. I encourage you, whether you are a female or a male, to identify your power and put it to good use. If someone or something has taken your power from you, reclaim it. The power of one can change situations for many on both an indirect and direct level.

Writing/Journal/Action/Discussion/Reflection Prompt:

What is an area that you would like to have power or more power than you currently possess? Write that power on a piece of paper and include how you want to use it for the betterment of another or others. Put that piece of paper somewhere that you can see it often throughout your day.

Day 19

You will never know until you try.

Have you ever stopped short of doing something because you were afraid that you would fail or fall below the projected target? I am certain that this has happened to everyone at some point. Possibly, you have started writing a book, placed one stroke upon a canvas, imagined trying-out for a team or group, thought about attending a college/university, conceived an idea for a business, or something else. In essence, you only took the first step in the process. Life is full of starts and fewer finishes. Turn your aspirations into possibilities by trying. You might be amazed at what awaits you at the finish.

Writing/Journal/Action/Discussion/Reflection Prompt:

What is the one thing that you are most afraid of starting because you think that you will not succeed at it? Now, imagine what will happen if you not only started but also finished the process. Make your thought a reality. Try!

Day 20

Trust your purpose.

You have within you a specific talent and purpose. In fact, you were born with that specific gift in order to carry out a certain mission. It is true that you might have more than one talent and several purposes. However, the key is in identifying your talent(s) and applying those to an area of existence in order to make "your difference" in the life of others. It can be a painstaking process to know your reason for being. However, if you are not willing to identify and apply your talent(s), you might miss-out on making "your difference." Do you truly not want to leave your imprint or make your impact? Have faith that if you want to know, you will find the direction.

Writing/Journal/Action/Discussion/Reflection Prompt:

What do you believe is your present purpose in life? Are you walking in the direction toward or away from that purpose? If you are walking toward, how can you make a positive difference in society? If you are walking away, how can you refocus and walk toward that purpose? Write your responses to these questions.

Day 21

You are an unstoppable force.

You have the ability to reach that goal and accomplish that dream. In ways, you are the only true force that can stop you from making it happen. Do not allow the discouraging words, actions, or thoughts of others get you off-track from allowing you to experience what can bring personal joy and happiness into your life. Listen to that inner voice and keep taking steps in the direction towards turning goals and dreams into reality.

Writing/Journal/Action/Discussion/Reflection Prompt:

What is something that you want to accomplish in the next two months? Write it down and put it somewhere that you can visibly see it daily. Each day, take positive steps and within 60 days, embrace what you did not permit others or circumstances to interfere happening for you.

Day 22

They told me I couldn't; that's why I did.

History is rampant with people who defied the odds. People who dared to do the unthinkable. Individuals as well as groups are often told, "You are not smart, old, or brave enough. You are not the right gender or race. That will never happen for someone like you." However, those very individuals and groups chose to ignore the negative influences, whether within or outside themselves, and do the "impossible." If you want to do something or become someone in life that others as well as you think is outside of your reach, go for it! Try it! The least of the possibilities is that you do not succeed or attain the level that you had hoped to attain. In that case, try again until you succeed.

Writing/Journal/Action/Discussion/Reflection Prompt:

Identify something that another or you believe that you cannot achieve. Identify three major steps that you must take in order to achieve. Put those steps into action. Within time, either evaluate the results and take new steps or relish in your success.

Day 23

Make it count.

It is a valid conclusion that everyone one gets one opportunity at life. Of course, there are those anomalies that "get a second chance at life" literally. Consequently, it is very important that you make the most of every moment that God gives you on Earth. You cannot recover lost time. Every second of every day, time moves forward. If you choose to stop and permit life to progress without taking part in the moments of the day, that is your choice. However, you just might miss an opportunity that you will never have again. Make the most of every moment.

Writing/Journal/Action/Discussion/Reflection Prompt:

Is there something/someone that you do not put your whole effort into in life? What is that something/someone? Identify and write about one significant way that you can begin to make that something/someone count in your life. Now, demonstrate that in your life.

Day 24

Be kind. Be fearless. Be you.

The Golden Rule should be a guiding principle in your everyday motives. Acts of kindness are essential to making the world a better place. Do not permit fear to stop you from showing kindness to a stranger or even someone who is not kind to you. Your gift or talent can positively affect the life of another. Choose to be the person that God requires you to be in life. One who is kind, courageous, and uniquely you.

Writing/Journal/Action/Discussion/Reflection Prompt:

List five ways in which you can be kind to another person, a thing, or the environment. Each day, try to incorporate one of these acts of kindness. The following day, incorporate a new way from your list. By the end of the week, you have been uniquely kind in five different ways. Repeat these manners each week. Within time, you will have incorporated intentional acts of kindness into you every day routine.

Day 25

Good things take time.

There is a reason that every living thing/being must undergo developmental stages. Every living thing and being by design must go through processes until reaching the maximum potential. In essence, this systematic approach applies to everything that you want to happen for yourself, someone else, or thing. Rarely do good things happen instantaneously. They take time. There is an order in which things happen. The process is most often one in which you do not have any control. Nevertheless, remain faithful and believe that you will receive what you have worked and waited to receive. Believe me!

Writing/Journal/Action/Discussion/Reflection Prompt:

What is one significant thing that you want to happen within the next six months? Put that hope or desire into writing. Write down key happenings during the process. Remember, be patient; you cannot give-up, and you must put in the effort to get the desired result.

Day 26

Follow your heart.

Within your heart resides a directional. If you listen closely to the beating, you will be steered along the right path. Realize that the path others take might not be the path for you. Actually, that should not be the focus. Your role is to listen and move. It knows where to take you.

Writing/Journal/Action/Discussion/Reflection Prompt:

In what way has your heart has pushed, pulled, or guided you? Take some time and pen it. Then, begin to walk in the direction that your heart leads you.

Day 27

Live your dream.

Whether, young or old and male or female, you have a dream for your present as well as your future. Dreams are the entry into what you want to become a reality in your life. It is possible that your dream will appear unattainable, especially when considering your present circumstances or situation. Nevertheless, you have to believe that what you foresee happening in your life can happen in your life, if you will it and take action. Dreams do and can come true. You are not an exception!

Writing/Journal/Action/Discussion/Reflection Prompt:

What is the most unattainable dream that you have for yourself? Be intentional and explore in written form how you can make that dream a reality, whether presently or in the future. Go after it.

Day 28

Create your own happiness.

Happiness is not something that you can purchase. It is not something that you can put on a shelf and save for a "rainy day." It is definitely not something that you can borrow from or transfer to another person. Happiness is something that you have to decide to experience, share, and explore every day of life. Happiness is not definitive. What brings happiness quickly and unexpectedly can bring the converse into your life. You might have to pursue happiness. However, once you obtain it, you must put in the effort necessary to permit it to flourish and control your life.

Writing/Journal/Action/Discussion/Reflection Prompt:

What brings you happiness? Is it a person, place, thing, idea, or a combination of these? Name whatever brings you joy into your life and go after your happy!

Day 29

one-of-a-kind

There is no other person living or deceased like you. You possess a genetic makeup that distinguishes you from anyone else. With that in mind, why would you want to be someone other than who you were designed to be? What harm exists in being an original? If others want to try to imitate you, let them try, but you are the only prototype of you. Be you and not someone else.

Writing/Journal/Action/Discussion/Reflection Prompt:

What does being you mean? Take a few minutes to think about this question. Create a list of at least 10 characteristics and/or gifts that make you uniquely you. Now, intentionally show others what makes you different from anyone else.

Day 30

Stop saying I wish; start saying I will.

Sometimes, the difference in hoping and becoming is between thinking and acting. To get what you want, you must transition from the conception phase to the achievement phase. Every human being wants more, desires change, and longs for turning what currently exists into something beyond the present. Whatever it is that you wish, stop imagining and carry-out the necessary tasks to make your wish a reality. Keep in mind, you might need the aid of others to make it happen for you.

Writing/Journal/Action/Discussion/Reflection Prompt:

What is at the top of your wish list? Devise a written plan for how you can make that wish come true in your life. Each week consult your plan and put it into action. Eventually, your dream is your reality.

Day 31

Live your story.

You have a story! You have a story! You have a story! You have a story, and it belongs to you. You might ask, "What is my story?" "What story do I have to live?" In fact, every day of your life you are living your story. Your story might not have begun the way that you would prefer, or your story presently might unfold in the manner that did not choose. Nevertheless, you are the author of your story. At any time, you have the authorship to alter or delete the existing storyline and create a new one. The goal is not to live someone else's story or story for you. You must live your own story.

Writing/Journal/Action/Discussion/Reflection Prompt:

What is your story? How would you like your story to end? Write your responses to these questions. Begin living what you have written for yourself.

Day 32

Live. Laugh. Love.

These three words permeate popular culture. Too often, people utter them without taking the time to ponder what these ideas/concepts truly mean. Even more so, fewer people authentically apply these words in their own life or in interactions with others. To live means to be present in the goings and comings of your everyday encounters. To laugh means to express joy outwardly so that others can see, hear, and know that living can bring happiness despite the present circumstances. To love means to demonstrate through words and actions genuine kindness, appreciation, and reverence for another being, place, or thing without knowledge of or regard for what might result.

Writing/Journal/Action/Discussion/Reflection Prompt:

Live, laugh, and love always! Identify some person, place, or thing that causes you to reflect each word in your life. Now, identify some person, place, or thing that does not cause you to reflect each word in your life. Consciously do something to change your response. This might take more time and effort than you would anticipate, but the purpose is to have genuine instances of living, laughing, and loving in your life daily.

Day 33

Beautiful minds inspire others.

The mind in all its wonder is amazing. Without your effort, it causes, creates, changes, compartmentalizes, cherishes, compels, and challenges. As the mind does these amazing things, you carryout these actions; others are often the direct and indirect recipients. Consequently, you have the potential to influence others in either a positive or a negative manner. You should want to influence your loved ones, friends, acquaintances, and even strangers toward dimensions that they might not be aware of in their life that will have a positive effect on them. No, it is not necessarily your responsibility to be the steward of another's life. However, what harm is it to use your mind to guide another in a rewarding rather than destructive direction?

Writing/Journal/Action/Discussion/Reflection Prompt:

Write about one specific way that you can use your mind positively to influence the life of another. Who is the individual? Implement this way in your day-to-day activities with them.

Day 34

You are perfect just the way you are.

Perfection is a goal that no one can attain. In fact, at no one point is it possible for anyone else or you to be free of flaws, physically or mentally. However, it is possible for you to accept yourself as you presently are and strive for improvement in any area that you deem improvement is necessary. Do not try to imitate another individual or model yourself after someone else's ideal of perfection. Every human being has flaws, imperfections, and limitations, even when attempting to be better human beings. Accept who you are at this moment. Acceptance is the true vision of perfection.

Writing/Journal/Action/Discussion/Reflection Prompt:

Who is someone that others or you identify as the perfect person? Why are they perfect? Are your reasons rooted in physical traits and characteristics? If so, identify intangible qualities that this person possesses that you can incorporate into your life. If not, identify intangible qualities that you admire and want to incorporate in your interactions within the world.

Day 35

(It's all about attitude.)

People believe that attitude determines aptitude. Whether you chose to view the world through rose tinted lenses or see the glass as half-empty, your perspective has influence on your potential. If you believe that you cannot do or achieve something, the reason might have roots in your perspective, whether the influence of another. Situations in life will not always go the way that you want or give you the option(s) that you hope to receive. Nevertheless, you do have the opportunity to control how you view the situations—positively, neutrally, or negatively.

Writing/Journal/Action/Discussion/Reflection Prompt:

List the ways that you deal with negative situations. List the ways you deal with positive situations? Closely consider your responses in both lists. Act. Focus on shortening your negative response list and respond neutrally or positively to life's situations.

Day 36

Love makes the world go round.

Love is healing. Love is infectious. Love is the source of kindness. Love is universal. In every way possible to everyone and everything everywhere, show and share your love.

Writing/Journal/Action/Discussion/Reflection Prompt:

What is one unique way that you show or share love? How can you extend that love to someone or something new?

Day 37

"…[L]ife, liberty, and the pursuit of happiness." – *US Declaration of Independence*

Justice. Equality. Diversity. Civil Rights. Equity. Freedom. Inclusion. Pleasure. Choice. Opportunity. Independence. Human Rights. Free Will. Joy.

Each of these words represent concepts. Concepts that symbolize the foundational ideals established by the Founding Fathers of the United States of America. Symbols that embody the words contained in the *United States Declaration of Independence*.

Writing/Journal/Action/Discussion/Reflection Prompt:

Which of these words resonate with you, whether in a positive or negative manner? In a detailed written explanation, share why these words either resonate or do not resonate with you. Include whether these words in the 21st century reflect or do not reflect the principles you believe this country represents for all people.

Day 38

The journey not the arrival matters.

Do you realize that in order to get to where you want to go you must take the first step? The first step leads to the second and then leads to all the steps that follow thereafter. Keep in mind, each step does not lead to or take you down a path that you have foreknowledge concerning. Rather, some steps will lead you toward detours, uncharted paths, and new adventures. The goal might be to reach your final destination by a certain time or at a certain point. Nevertheless, the goal sometimes becomes to keep moving, moving in a forward direction. Along the way, you will experience situations, people, places, and things that will strengthen you, make you wiser, and provide new perspectives. Persevere. You will eventually reach the destination that is the best for you given that point in life.

Writing/Journal/Action/Discussion/Reflection Prompt:

Write your interpretation of "The journey not the arrival matters."

Day 39

Just be you.

You are the only person who can be you. You were specifically crafted, created, and birth to be you and no one else. If others choose, let them be imitators. You are the original! You are uniquely you!

Writing/Journal/Action/Discussion/Reflection Prompt:

Why is it difficult being you sometimes? Truly take some time to reflect on this question. Write all of the thoughts that come to your mind. Identify responses that are within your control to change and make conscious effort to change them now! You deserve to be you!

Day 40

Explore.

Open yourself to new opportunity, the unknown, foreign, forgotten. Doing so just might lead to new adventures. Exploration is the mother of invention. Invent a new experience for yourself. You do not know what awaits you at the onset, during, or afterward. Dare to step towards uncharted territory in your life.

Writing/Journal/Action/Discussion/Reflection Prompt:

What is someplace or something that you are hesitant, whether because of someone else's experience or fear, to explore? What is holding you back from exploring? Devise a plan that will lead to your new discovery, whether about yourself, someone, some thing, or some place.

Day 41

(What you think is what you say!)

What is on your mind is most often what comes out of your mouth. You should always want what you say aloud and/or to and about others to reflect your true feelings and perceptions. It is possible that what you are thinking if uttered will be negative to the receiver(s). Nevertheless, if you have taken time to think about the consequence, potential offense, and situation that your words might provoke, your words might be the necessary catalyst to bring about a positive outcome. Next time, be intentional with your words and speak your truth because people need to know and you have the right to express what is on your mind. Your words just might start a movement.

Writing/Journal/Action/Discussion/Reflection Prompt:

What is on your mind that you have been cautious to share? Write it down and express why you have been cautious.

Day 42

(50% hard work + 50% perseverance = 100% success.)

Hard work and perseverance are the keys to success. Most things that you really want to happen in life will not result from minimal to no effort. Everything that you want to accomplish requires effort and commitment. The level of effort and commitment will vary dependent upon the desired outcome. Nevertheless, if you begin any pursuit by giving at least half of each, the only possibility is for the outcome to fall somewhere of the success scale.

Writing/Journal/Action/Discussion/Reflection Prompt:

What is something that you know you have not given the necessary level of effort or commitment? What more can you do now so that you reach the success that you desire?

Day 43

Your attitude determines your direction.

A negative attitude leads you in the wrong direction. A positive attitude leads you in the right direction. If you do not think this to be true, begin to pay attention to individuals who you believe have negative attitudes as well as those who have positive attitudes. Rarely does a positive attitude lead you in the wrong direction and vice versa. It is possible that you are not going down your preferred path(s). If this is the case, become more aware of your thoughts, which directly affect your attitude.

Writing/Journal/Action/Discussion/Reflection Prompt:

Do you believe that you have a positive or negative attitude? Which of the two would your family or friends associate with you? Evaluate both perspectives—yours and others—and think in the direction that you want your life to go.

Day 44

One small positive thought in the morning can change your whole day.

The mind is a powerful tool. Positive thinking is just one fraction of the numerous capabilities of the mind at any time. If you wake up on the "wrong side of the bed," optimistic thinking can turn a dismal day or situation into a promising day or situation. Any foreseen or unforeseen situation can cause you to revert to negative thought. Consequently, you likely will have to exercise this practice more than one time during the day. View life's happenings with a positive outlook because your thoughts have a power to influence your actions.

Writing/Journal/Action/Discussion/Reflection Prompt:

Write about a time in your life when you permitted a negative thought to affect your entire day. Include one positive thought that could have opposed your negative thought, which might have led to a better day or outcome.

Day 45

Smile.

It is certain that you will experience unhappy and uncomfortable moments as well as periods in your life, but smiling is an exercise that invites people, positive energy, and opportunity into your life. The next time that life is not going the way that you prefer, spend more time smiling than frowning. It takes fewer muscles to smile than it does to frown.

Writing/Journal/Action/Discussion/Reflection Prompt:

Intentionally, smile throughout the day. At the end of the day, write about your day and share how others responded to you (smiling).

Day 46

(Use your voice for good!)

You live at a moment in human existence when people possibly more than ever choose to (publicly) use their voice: to uplift and to cast down; to advocate and to oppose; to accept and to judge; to approve and to condemn; to offer and to deny; to create and to destroy; to promote and to impede; to align and to separate; to be a friend and to be a foe.

Writing/Journal/Action/Discussion/Reflection Prompt:

How will you use your voice? Share in a details your response to this question.

Day 47

Dream. Imagine. Believe.

The world is full of opportunity. Opportunity that is waiting for you to fathom such a possibility for your life. Possibility that has the potential to become your reality. Reality that awaits your awareness of your today and your tomorrow. Tomorrow, you must continue to hope will be better than today. Today is when you must dream, imagine, and believe in what appears to be impossible.

Writing/Journal/Action/Discussion/Reflection Prompt:

What is something that you believe is not possible, but if given the opportunity, you would seize? Write about this response with respect to short-term and long-term possibility.

Day 48

(What you believe is what you live!)

Do you believe the thoughts that you have about yourself less or more than the thoughts that others believe about you? Do you believe that people are inherently good, worthy, and unselfish, or that people are inherently evil, unworthy, and selfish? Do you believe that the world is the best that it will ever be or that it can be a better place? Your responses to these questions indicate your beliefs. Each day, you live out your beliefs, whether directly or indirectly. Your beliefs are influenced by people (family, friends, enemies, and strangers), media (print, Internet, television, and mobile devices), concepts (spirituality, diversity, inequity, and culture), and environment (social, familial, community, and global). Be very careful when deciding what people, things, ideas, and places influence your beliefs because your beliefs will direct the way you live.

Writing/Journal/Action/Discussion/Reflection Prompt:

What is one significant belief that you possess and you are living out that belief on a daily basis? Is this belief rooted in fairness or bias? Include if that belief does/could aid or hinder the life, liberty, and the pursuit of happiness for another individual?

Day 49

Be the best version of you.

There will never be another person born into the world who is 100% you. With all of your talents, traits, characteristics, dreams, potential, and so much more, you were destined to become the person that you are and continue to become each day. You were not crafted to be someone else or what someone else wants you to become. Neither strive nor settle for less than the 100% version of you.

Writing/Journal/Action/Discussion/Reflection Prompt:

What is one reason why you believe that you should strive to be the best version of yourself?

Day 50

Enjoy the little things.

No everything that happens is worth shouting from the rooftop. Somethings a noteworthy. Somethings are mere happenings. Regardless of the magnitude, severity, intensity, or impact, you should take time to appreciate, relish, celebrate, and reflect upon the occurrences in other's and your own life. By noticing the simpler occurrences, you are more likely to celebrate the more involved occurrences throughout life.

Writing/Journal/Action/Discussion/Reflection Prompt:

What has happened in your life that you found to be trivial and unworthy of celebrating? What influenced your decision to not take time to enjoy the little things? How can you begin to celebrate all occurrences, great and small?

Day 51

(Shine your light daily.)

You have a personal aura. It is often noticed by others and rarely by you. It is in ways like a force that is unique only to you, and it affects those with whom you come in contact. When someone is down, your aura has the potential to lift their spirit. At times of despair, your aura can instill hope. In other words, shine your light daily. It does not matter if the way or room is already lit, your light brings with it added energy that someone needs, today.

Writing/Journal/Action/Discussion/Reflection Prompt:

Are you fearful of shining your light for others to see? Why or why not?

Day 52

(Words matter.)

Words have POWER! You should always be thoughtful and intentional when using your words. Once words escape your mind and are captured in written or spoken (or gestured) form, they have been received by another. Never say something that you do not mean. Words are not able to be "unsent" or "unreceived." Whether the message it not the most sensitive, comfortable, or timely; is rooted from a place of pain, anger, or confusion; is reflective of your truth, your experience, or your feelings, SAY it, WRITE it, and MEAN it! Your words have the power to bring about necessary change.

Writing/Journal/Action/Discussion/Reflection Prompt:

Write a poem or letter in which you use your words intentionally to convey the truth as you see/know it! Share your poem or letter with another person.

Day 53

All things are possible.

Belief. Hope. Faith. Determination. Trust. These are essential variables in calling into being those things that are presently not your reality. Take time daily to meditate on and pray for situations to change in your life. Do not will negativity; this is a counterproductive act. Remember, you must rely upon the five aforementioned words throughout the period of mediation and prayer. At the designated moment, what was not will become that which is in your life.

Writing/Journal/Action/Discussion/Reflection Prompt:

What is something that you want that is presently only a possibility? Align your thinking and actions so that what you want can come into or be in your life.

Day 54

(Believe it, and you will achieve it.)

A large degree of accomplishment exists in the power of belief. When you believe, you take something that is passive and place it in the realm of active. There are countless individuals, living and deceased, within society for whom belief was essential in bringing forth some form of change. Joan of Arc, Harriett Tubman, Frederick Douglass, Theodore Roosevelt, Nelson and Winnie Mandela, Mahatma Gandhi, Mother Theresa, Paolo Freire, Malcolm X, Dr. and Mrs. Martin Luther King, Jr., Toni Morrison, Thurgood Marshall, Mr. and Mrs. Loving, Spike Lee, John F. Kennedy, Jr., César Chavez, (former) Congressman John Lewis, Stephen Spielberg, Oprah Winfrey, and numerous individuals had a belief that propelled them forward. The change that these individuals sought did not only influence their immediate audience/community but also influenced the world. Despite adversity and opposition, these individuals moved their perception into action. Make no comparisons. Step into your destiny driven by belief. Along the path, you just might change a person, a community, or the world.

Writing/Journal/Action/Discussion/Reflection Prompt:

What is something that you have a strong belief and want to implement for positive change? Find someone living or deceased that had a similar belief and study his or her steps. Now, begin turning your passive stance into an active stance.

Day 55

(Imagine your tomorrow today.)

You have a future. You might not know that now because you possibly can neither see nor fathom it, and your future can be better than your today. If no one else reminds you of this, you must remind yourself. What you want can be yours. However, you have to create an image of your tomorrow in your mind. You have to daily work at making your creation your reality. Regardless of how realistic your image for your future is in the mind of others as well as yourself. The future is no more than 24 hours away.

Writing/Journal/Action/Discussion/Reflection Prompt:

Have you ever given much thought to tomorrow? Well, if not, begin today. It is well within reason to write your thoughts about your future.

Day 56

(Think better. Do better. Be better.)

Have you ever heard the statement, "You are what you think?" This statement aligns with the quote for today. Working towards personal improvement should be a constant effort in your life. However, improvement is not something that automatically happens for anyone. You must bring into line your thoughts and your actions. If you think about volunteering for an organization so that you can make matters better for the population that it services, you must go beyond thought. You must seek out a means by which you can volunteer. By giving selflessly of yourself, volunteering, you are directly working towards personal improvement. You can be a better person, but it extends beyond thought.

Writing/Journal/Action/Discussion/Reflection Prompt:

What is one area in which you would like to improve? Why do you believe that you need to improve in this area? Who is an individual/What is an organization that can help you in this process? You have thought about it. Now, do something about it. These are the first two steps towards personal improvement.

Day 57

(Pause, think, then respond.)

Do not be so eager to respond to stimuli, whether verbal or visual. It is a best practice to take a few moments before reacting. Those few moments might be the difference between escalation and de-escalation, failure and success, and wrong and right. The other person(s) and you deserve that added moment of your time.

Writing/Journal/Action/Discussion/Reflection Prompt:

Are you someone who thinks about what they want to say before saying it? If so, why do you wait? If not, why do you not wait? How can you consciously begin or continue implementing a wait-time before responding or reacting to others?

Day 58

Love.

For some people, love is a simple task that requires minimal forethought, especially when demonstrated towards the familiar. As proof of its simplicity, love is a demonstration of reverence, appreciation, and respect for another person, animal, or thing. For others, love is a complex emotion, and it is rarely displayed or shown towards another. As proof of its complexity, the ancient Greeks identified three forms of love: Eros (romantic), Philia (brotherly), and Agape (universal). Whether you view love as simple, complex, or a combination of both, the world is in need of your love. Do not wait!

Writing/Journal/Action/Discussion/Reflection Prompt:

Find an opportunity to show love, every day.

Day 59

With all your heart.

Never do something half-heartedly. Give all that you have within you to whatever it is that you do. Your heart can handle the load.

Writing/Journal/Action/Discussion/Reflection Prompt:

Write about a time when you did not give all of your heart to accomplish a task, meet a goal, or fulfil a dream. Moving forward what will be the benefit of using your whole heart?

Day 60

Open mind 24/7.

When you possess a closed mind, you limit your experiences. Throughout life, you will encounter all types of people, places, things, and ideas. Some of your encounters will provide opportunities for you to awaken to things that you have neither had exposure to nor imagined possible. Nevertheless, it is most definite that you should not be open to permitting anyone, anything, or any message to sway you away from any belief or practice that you deem not harmful and not rooted in biases, prejudices, and stereotypes. An open mind does not mean that you permit thoughts that are unkind, unjust, and unsound room to grow within you. Rather, an open mind means that you welcome difference, variety, and new experiences that can help strengthen your existing thought patterns and cause you to question those that stunt your mental, spiritual, and (inter)personal growth.

Writing/Journal/Action/Discussion/Reflection Prompt:

To what do you possess a closed mind? Why do you possess this stance? Is there any possibility that you might be open to alternative perspectives? Please consider these questions in a detailed written response.

Day 61

Think. Learn.

The mind performs one intricate process and that is to think. When you think, you allow your body, specifically, your brain to operate as designed. When you think, you allow synapses to form as you make connections between your thoughts and your reality. Thinking is possibly the most essential component of the learning process. In order to receive, retain, and reiterate information, you both must consciously and subconsciously think about the information that transmits to your brain. Through the process of comprehending, analyzing, evaluating, and synthesizing, you take the knowledge that you obtain and further make connections. Always choose to be a thinker and a learner.

Writing/Journal/Action/Discussion/Reflection Prompt:

Identify something that you need/want to think about more often. Take some time to learn (more) about the object of your thoughts. You might discover some compelling information, which could promote further thinking and learning.

Day 62

Dream.

The art of imagining rooted in reality.

Writing/Journal/Action/Discussion/Reflection Prompt:

What is something that you dream about more than other things? Explore why you dream about this as much as you do, possibly there exists a deeper purpose to your dreaming.

Day 63

Live! Time waits for no one.

Every moment time lapses forward, whether measured in seconds, minutes, hours, days, weeks, months, or years. If you decide to wait until a situation improves or until a pending decision is made, you might miss-out on something significant often called "living." Regardless if you choose to act, be still, or wait, time ticks onward, the hands on the clock progress from A.M. to P.M., day becomes night, weeks become months, and one more birthday is added to your tally, and you have neither done nor accomplished for another year that one thing. Before another year passes, take time out to actively participate in life. Being passive should not be an option.

Writing/Journal/Action/Discussion/Reflection Prompt:

What is something that you have waited to accomplish? List five steps that you can actively take within the next 30 to 60 days to get closer to making it happen sooner rather than later.

Day 64

Follow your arrow.

Every arrow has a trajectory once released from its bow. Every person has a path to follow once beginning life's journey. The purpose of the arrow is to reach the target. The purpose of a person is to fulfill their destiny. Be like the arrow, follow your purpose and hit your target.

Writing/Journal/Action/Discussion/Reflection Prompt:

In what direction is your arrow sending you? What are (potential) interferences that might redirect your arrow? What can you do to prepare for or avoid the (potential) interferences?

Day 65

Make your dreams happen.

If you do not, who will? Others are only able to assist you in the process. Fundamentally, it is up to you to do everything within your ability to turn your mental imaginings into real-life happenings.

Writing/Journal/Action/Discussion/Reflection Prompt:

What dream are you presently pursuing?

Day 66

All you need is love.

Love is life's miracle elixir. If administered with care, love heals wounds, mends hurts, and rights wrongs. Love is the cure for many of the ailments and ills within people and society.

Writing/Journal/Action/Discussion/Reflection Prompt:

Find someone who is in need of love and share your love with them?

Day 67

(Do something!)

Life is an action word. What you encounter is not by accident or mere coincidence. When you witness, observe, see, feel, or think, it is obligatory that you act. Regardless of the magnitude of your response, your action will make some positive degree of difference even if you think otherwise. Doing nothing should never be an option.

Writing/Journal/Action/Discussion/Reflection Prompt:

What is something that compels you to want to do something, possibly in a manner that you have never done? How can you take action? Strongly consider these questions and then move forward into that direction.

Day 68

All things grow with love.

As sun is to every living thing so is love to every living being. Sun provides the required nutrients for plants to maintain health and produce oxygen to feed the world. Love fosters the environment for people to feel meaningful and cultivates the need to reciprocate to other beings. Never underestimate the necessity of love in your life, as you should never undervalue the requirement of sun to living things.

Writing/Journal/Action/Discussion/Reflection Prompt:

What is something that you have denied love, whether intentionally or unintentionally?

Day 69

Gratitude is the best attitude.

Give thanks! Being gracious does not cost you anything. Being gracious does not take much time. Being gracious puts you in a posture for receiving grace. You can show gratitude through gestures, words, tangibles, and acts. When in doubt, give thanks!

Writing/Journal/Action/Discussion/Reflection Prompt:

Have you thanked someone today? Take some time to let someone know how grateful you are for their presence in your life.

Day 70

Hope changes everything.

Hopelessness is the opposite of hope. For whatever reason, you might feel hopeless today. Hopelessness is worry. You might be experiencing a sense that some situation will not workout in your favor. If that statement describes you, look upward. Gaze into the large expanse called "sky." What do you see? Do you see clouds and a sun or stars and a moon? Really, what you see or do not see is not of no consequence. What really matters is that these things exist without worry. You too exist, and worry should not pervade your existence, today or any other day. Let go of worry and choose hope.

Writing/Journal/Action/Discussion/Reflection Prompt:

What is something for which you need hope? Identify two ways that you can turn this hopelessness into hope.

Day 71

You got this!

You are equipped at this very moment to handle your current situation. Step-out and do what you were born to do in life at this time.

Writing/Journal/Action/Discussion/Reflection Prompt:

What is something that you can handle? Explain how and why you are prepared for it.

Day 72

Strive for progress not perfection.

Perfection is a destructive word. It causes you to compare and contrast yourself to someone else. It causes you to pursue things that realistically do not exist. Through that evaluation process, you often disqualify yourself from being and doing because you think that you will not be good enough. Release yourself from that type of thinking. It is a goal that no one can attain, including you. As long as you are moving forward and doing the best that you can, you are making progress.

Writing/Journal/Action/Discussion/Reflection Prompt:

Do you believe that striving for perfection is attainable? Why or why not?

Day 73

Life is beautiful.

Beauty surrounds you. From the moment that you awaken to the moment that you sleep, you have many opportunities to experience beauty. Do not take life or the moments it affords you to witness beauty.

Writing/Journal/Action/Discussion/Reflection Prompt:

Do you consider your life to be beautiful? Write about one reason as to why you do or why you do not.

Day 74

Imagine. Create. Inspire.

Think the extraordinary. Create the never before seen. Inspire the forgotten. You unlike anyone. Use your conceptions to form and to motivate others. What others have done should not be a factor. What you were created to do is what matters most.

Writing/Journal/Action/Discussion/Reflection Prompt:

What is one thing you imagine? What is one creation that you would like to design? In what way would you like to inspire others?

Day 75

Home is where your story begins.

Home is where most people have their foundation. It is often where many firsts in life take place, especially one's first learning environment. Home is where you begin to see the world from a common point of view, which later becomes a perspective all your own. For many people, home is a familiar, safe, and nurturing place. Perhaps, your experiences of home are a contrast to these. Either way, no other individual's perspective of home is exactly like your perspective, even if you shared the same address.

Writing/Journal/Action/Discussion/Reflection Prompt:

Write about the place where your story began.

Day 76

(Failure is not an option.)

You were not born with the presumption that you were not meant to experience success, victory, triumph, and achievement. However, you were born with the understanding that life would not always bring moments of bliss, satisfaction, positivity, and goodness. It is your responsibility to not allow the less comfortable and more challenging moments and experiences in life to stop you from moving forward or moving towards some hoped outcome. Rather than view obstacles as failures, view them as setbacks or delays along your journey. Always remember, a setback or a delay does not mean an end. You can obtain that goal, reach that outcome, and gain that intrinsic and/or extrinsic reward, if you do not accept disappointment.

Writing/Journal/Action/Discussion/Reflection Prompt:

What is something that others or you have viewed as a defeat in your life? How can you turn that perception or experience into a win?

Day 77

Faith makes all things possible.

Hope. Belief. Trust. Reliance. These are synonyms for faith. When all that you have tried is to no avail, do not give up. Persevere with hope, belief, trust, reliance, and faith. You will ultimately see the possibilities.

Writing/Journal/Action/Discussion/Reflection Prompt:

What is something in someone else's or your life that you need faith?

Day 78

Think happy. Be happy.

Dopamine, serotonin, oxytocin, and endorphins are the chemicals released from your brain that produce happiness. Rather than being unhappy, involve yourself in those things that bring happiness. Simply stated, happy thoughts lead to a happy being (and a happy existence).

Writing/Journal/Action/Discussion/Reflection Prompt:

What brings you happiness and why?

Day 79

Don't let anyone dull your sparkle.

You might be an individual to whom others often gravitate towards. You might possess a positive self-image often noticed by others. You might exude positive energy to the extent that others' spirits lift because of your presence. In essence, people might notice your personal glow. Others might speak negatively, take offense, and express envy. Let your light shine!

Writing/Journal/Action/Discussion/Reflection Prompt:

Has anyone ever made you feel as if your glow was too bright? Explain. Have you ever tried to dim someone else's glow? Explain.

Day 80

Cherish today.

Why do you take for granted the opportunities placed before you each day? Why do you wait until the next opportunity presents itself to you? Why do you wait to make amends with the people you hurt or hurt you; say hello to the person that you see every day who smiles at you as you pass by them; or show the people in your life how much they truly mean to you? Your tomorrow is no guarantee. Treasure the now.

Writing/Journal/Action/Discussion/Reflection Prompt:

What is one way that you will seize this day?

Day 81

Be YOU tiful

You are beautiful in all ways. Race, size; ethnicity; gender; age; unique; nationality; minority; religion; socio-economic; culture; (dis)ability; language; common; talent; and diverse. These are only a minute fraction of all the ways that make you beautifully you. Embrace and represent your beauty.

Writing/Journal/Action/Discussion/Reflection Prompt:

What is one way in which you believe that you are beautiful? Describe in detail how, why, and if this perspective is viewed as positive or negative by others?

Day 82

There are so many beautiful reasons to be happy.

Firstly, you have been given another day of life. Secondly, you are able to appreciate all that this day affords you. Thirdly, you have the opportunity to begin, continue, or complete something that you waited for until today. Find your happiness.

Writing/Journal/Action/Discussion/Reflection Prompt:

What is the most significant reason for your happiness? Share your response with someone else.

Day 83

Live each day with a grateful heart.

Giving thanks should be a natural component of everyone's personal etiquette. Being grateful is an expression of your gratitude for another person's generosity. As you outwardly show appreciation, you inwardly create positive energy that improves your well-being and health. A grateful heart is one that should be worn on your sleeve.

Writing/Journal/Action/Discussion/Reflection Prompt:

List two ways that you show gratitude? Identify one new way to show gratitude.

Day 84

Enjoy little things.

Life abounds with occasions. You as do many people probably look forward to those occasions that are more momentous than others. In the waiting period from one major event to the next, you fail to notice the minor occurrences. Certainly, you can think of those on your own. All the same, appreciate the less significant moments in between the most significant moments. Those moments just might hold more significance than you thought they would in life.

Writing/Journal/Action/Discussion/Reflection Prompt:

What is something that you deem as insignificant that in retrospect you can view as significant in your life? Discuss why your perspective has changed.

Day 85

Sorry... Yesterday was the deadline for all complaints.

Are you an individual who could be identified as a consummate objector? Do you too often find fault with most things, people, and situations? Could many of your criticisms be considered unreasonable? Well, the edict is out. If you cannot find an objection within 24 hours, keep your objection to yourself. After the fact disgruntlement will no longer be permissible.

Writing/Journal/Action/Discussion/Reflection Prompt:

What is one way to help curb the appetite of a constant complainer? If you consider yourself or others consider you to be a complainer, what purpose do your objections serve in any given matter?

Day 86

Keep smiling.

Do not let life, people, places, things, or ideas steal your joy! Smiling is a positive form of non-verbal communication. Smiling lifts moods. Smiling is compelling. Smiling is good for both the bearer and the receiver.

Writing/Journal/Action/Discussion/Reflection Prompt:

Who is someone who has smiled through the pains of life, or have you ever smiled though the pains in life? What motivated them or you to keep smiling?

Day 87

Dance like no one is watching. Sing like no one is listening.

Too often in life, you might not do something due to fear of being noticed by someone else. If something brings you joy or is a thought on a whim, do what can lighten your mood, can bring you joy, and do what you feel. You never know who might be watching or listening to you that gets inspired by your throwing caution to the wind.

Writing/Journal/Action/Discussion/Reflection Prompt:

What is something that you would like to do if no one is watching? Do it!

Day 88

Nothing is going to change my world.

You are unmovable, steadfast, and strongminded. No force, person, thing, or concept is going to reposition you. You are confident in your beliefs, practices, and perceptions. You have a clearly defined path upon which your feet are firmly set. You are going to accomplish that thing that you set out to achieve, whether today or tomorrow or in the near or in the distant future.

Writing/Journal/Action/Discussion/Reflection Prompt:

What is one belief that no one can make you change your mind? Explain why you cannot be swayed.

Day 89

(Be open to new adventures.)

The familiar breeds complacency. Stepping out into something new can be unnerving. For most people, change is an unwelcomed sign that things will be different. Fortunately, not all change is negative. Change, while inevitable, can be inviting and invigorating. Change can lead you toward outcomes that you possibly would not experience if circumstances remained the same. The next time that change knocks on your door, open the door and welcome the new adventure.

Writing/Journal/Action/Discussion/Reflection Prompt:

Are you hesitant to change? Explain why or why not.

Day 90

The secret ingredient is always love.

For this recipe, you will need the following ingredients: empathy, acceptance, humility, patience, sensitivity, and respect. Once you have blended each of these ingredients, add the most important one, love. Without love, the outcome will be less than predestined.

Writing/Journal/Action/Discussion/Reflection Prompt:

Do you believe that love is the most essential factor in life? Write why or why not and include examples to support your choice.

Day 91

Every moment matters.

When you are at a standstill, you are experiencing a moment. A moment can be of varying lengths of time. The most significant aspect of a moment lies in the decision that you make within that duration. During that period, you must make the decision as to how you will proceed and transition from that point to the next. The decision that you make is important and determines where you go next, with whom or what you interact, and the impact to life's trajectory.

Writing/Journal/Action/Discussion/Reflection Prompt:

Describe a moment in your life in which you did not make the most productive use of your time. How did that decision affect your moving forward?

Day 92

Let your ideas bloom.

You have glorious thoughts regardless of what anyone else believes or states. Whether they are in the beginning phase or completely planned, your thoughts have the potential to become marvelous ideas. Give worth to your thoughts. Your thoughts might develop into the ideas that better society.

Writing/Journal/Action/Discussion/Reflection Prompt:

What is one idea that you cannot remove for your mind? Identify two ways that you can further develop that idea. Seek out individuals that you trust who can assist you.

Day 93

Believe.

When you believe, you consciously choose to place a value of truth to that thing, place, idea, or person. During life, your beliefs will adjust based upon your direct and indirect experiences. Consequently, it is important that you establish a sound belief system that is rooted in principles and practices that you deem essential for quality living. Try not to permit biases and stereotypes to influence you; however, it is only logical that they will have some level of impact. If this is your claim, I believe what I believe. Find usefulness in that belief or change it.

Writing/Journal/Action/Discussion/Reflection Prompt:

In what/Where are your beliefs rooted?

Day 94

Open a book. Open your mind.

Reading is like time traveling. It transports you to places and times, whether remote or nearby; of the past, present, or future. Reading is like having the opportunity to live someone else's experiences. The act of reading permits you to become your favorite protagonist or antagonist; enables you to walk in another person's footsteps, and allows you to live vicariously through another. Reading is like peering into the mind of an author. Why have you not grabbed/found that book and started reading it?

Writing/Journal/Action/Discussion/Reflection Prompt:

What is an area or subject that you would like to know more than you presently know? Find, borrow, or buy the book that discusses, explores, or expresses your interest. Then, find a place to read.

Day 95

Live the life you imagined.

There exists no guarantee for any time on Earth beyond this moment. Considerably, why would you choose to live it any way other than the way that you have dreamed to live your life? If you never spend time considering the possible paths that you could travel along your journey on Earth, please take or make the time. Your life depends upon it!

Writing/Journal/Action/Discussion/Reflection Prompt:

What is the life that you imagined for yourself? Are you living, working on living, or far from living the life that you imagined? Provide a detailed explanation.

Day 96

"Do the best you can until you know better. Then when you know better, do better." Maya Angelou

Life is about learning from your achievements and your mistakes. Hopefully, you realize that you were not born with all the information that you need to navigate throughout life. Furthermore, it is not the expectation that you learn it all before you leave home and enter and interact with the systems within the world. Rather, it is through directly and indirectly lived experiences that you build upon your foundation—values, beliefs, ideals, and practices. Continuously, you identify what works and what does not work and ultimately what is best for society and you. Do not allow others as well as yourself to be too harsh when you make those mistakes in life because the hope is that you learn from them and adjust your foundation in preparation for the achievement.

Writing/Journal/Action/Discussion/Reflection Prompt:

What is one truth that you learned as a result of making a mistake, once, twice, or more? How have you applied what you learned as you moved forward?

Day 97

In a world where you can be anything, be yourself.

It is evident that most people aspire to a certain role or title at some point in their life. In your attainment of that role or title, do not get spellbound and try to become the person or people associated with that role or title. Be yourself as you work towards, after attainment, and until the end of that role or title. The world deserves you!

Writing/Journal/Action/Discussion/Reflection Prompt:

Have you ever tried to be someone else? Why or why not?

Day 98

Breathe in. Breathe out. Repeat.

Have you ever felt like you were losing control, overwhelmed, or like a rug was pulled from underneath your feet in a situation? You are not alone. In those or similar moments, the best course of action is to follow the above noted statement. It really does work.

Writing/Journal/Action/Discussion/Reflection Prompt:

What is your primary method discreetly to use to gain control of a situation? Why do you use this method? How effective is it?

Day 99

Old ways won't open new doors.

The world is forever changing. As a human being, you should want to adapt to those changes. Adaption is a crucial component of the evolution of the human being. No one must require you to relinquish all of your former ways of thinking, being, and doing. However, being static and closed-off to change is neither realistic nor logical. It is obvious that you want to progress throughout life, and by doing so, you must prepare for the doors that will open for you.

Writing/Journal/Action/Discussion/Reflection Prompt:

Why are people resistant to change? Think of and explain one specific area for which you believe and have witnessed this to be true?

Day 100

Dream big. Laugh lots. Love life.

Take an active role in your lived experiences. It is crucial that you play a part in every moment that is given to you. Do not simply exist. When fathoming the things that potentially lie ahead for you, think realistically but think on a grander scale and step outside the walls that presently limit your possibilities. Find joy in all things and express your happiness in outward displays. Emotions affect your experiences and what better experience is there than a positive, beneficial, and uplifting. While living, be certain to show charity, appreciation, and admiration for humanity and all representations of creation.

Writing/Journal/Action/Discussion/Reflection Prompt:

Identify and write about one way that you will significantly apply today's statement during the coming week.

Day 101

Be a voice not an echo.

Do you believe that you have something of significance to say? Do you believe that an urge within compels you to express what is on your mind and your heart? Do you believe that there exist more voices that sound the same? Do you believe that the voice that stands for difference still is to be heard? Do you believe that you are a voice for change? Find your issue, stand upon your chosen platform, and boldly proclaim your truth. The world is waiting to hear your voice.

Writing/Journal/Action/Discussion/Reflection Prompt:

What is something that you want to say but fear and other voices have caused you to blend in with the crowd? State that desire and provide in detail how you will share it with others.

Day 102

Stop wishing; start doing.

A wish is a desire for an expected result. If you do put action to your desire, not only will you begin moving in the direction that you want, but also you will reach your expected result. Waiting for tomorrow or another individual is not sufficient, you must begin today.

Writing/Journal/Action/Discussion/Reflection Prompt:

What is one thing that you wish to happen? Begin today by putting a desire into motion.

Day 103

Be kind. No exceptions.

Cruelty, hatred, envy, malice, spite, and heartless are antonyms for kindness. With all your might, remove these vices from your mind, vocabulary, and actions. The world has too many examples of unkindness on a daily basis. Without doubt, God created you to love your enemy and friend, to treat a stranger as you would a guest, and to show humanity to all kind, whether far or near and different or similar. If not you, then who else?

Writing/Journal/Action/Discussion/Reflection Prompt:

Have you ever expected someone else to be kind in a situation when you were not kind? Why should a double standard exist for you?

Day 104

Love always wins.

In a struggle between positive and negative forces, positive always wins. Faith wins over fear. Kindness wins over hatred. Unity wins over division. Good wins over evil. Love wins over hate. It might not appear that way at first, remain certain, stay the course, and see that in the end, positivity prevails.

Writing/Journal/Action/Discussion/Reflection Prompt:

Think of a time in history, win love (a positive force) won over hate (a negative force)? Who/what represented love and hate? What force prevailed at the end of the battle? Why do you think this force won?

Day 105

Family is forever.

What does family mean to you? You might recognize family as genetically related individuals. You might name family as a father, mother, and offspring. You might name family as individuals legally connected or an assumed unit. You might describe a family as a group of people who display love (and hate) towards one another. You might even believe that a family is a group of individuals with no specific connection. Whatever description that you prefer, whatever connection that you associate, whatever circumstances exist or do not exist, you are your family, and your family is you.

Writing/Journal/Action/Discussion/Reflection Prompt:

In what ways are you connected to your family? Explain.

Day 106

Sometimes you win. Sometimes you learn.

Not every situation in life is a competition. Respectively, you cannot expect to always reign victorious. Even the most prepared and deft experience the possibility of loss and defeat. Do not approach life from a win or lose perspective. Rather, approach life from a win or learn perspective. Ironically, even in loss and defeat, you can learn something about yourself that you did not know previously that can strengthen your resolve and add to your character. Consequently, the next time that you are in a competition and the results do not go in your favor, consider it a "learn" and not a loss.

Writing/Journal/Action/Discussion/Reflection Prompt:

Name an instance in your life when you learned something rather than loss in a competition? How do you grow/could you have grown from this learning experience?

Day 107

Believe in yourself.

If you do not, who do you expect will believe in you?

Writing/Journal/Action/Discussion/Reflection Prompt:

Do you believe in yourself? Why is it important to have faith in yourself?

Day 108

Follow your dreams, they somehow know the way.

Do you ever feel lost? Do you ever feel as if everyone else appears to know where they are going but not you? Do you ever think that you are on the right path only to realize sometime later that it is not the best one? Is it possible that you are ignoring the thoughts that are directing you because they seem unrealistic and unattainable? One suggestion is that the next time one of those thoughts return, take a moment to consider its possibility. There might be more value to it than you initially understood.

Writing/Journal/Action/Discussion/Reflection Prompt:

Where do you want to go? What do you want to do? What imaginings have you had and how can they aid you in getting there?

Day 109

(Love actually is all around us.)

You can show love with words, actions, and thoughts. A thank you note, a conversation, a poem conversation; an opened door for a stranger, a home-cooked meal, a smile; charity, acceptance, equity. The representations are endless. Open your eyes. Open your heart. Open your mind.

Writing/Journal/Action/Discussion/Reflection Prompt:

Which of the three ways to show love is the easiest for you? Why? Provide an example in your response.

Day 110

Let your faith be bigger than your fear.

No one person is devoid of fear or the impairing symptoms of it. Fear is a natural and necessary part of life's experiences because no one is 100% fearless. However, fear can consume you. It can cause you to remain stationary when everyone and everything around you is in constant motion. It can steal spiritually, physically, mentally, emotionally, financially, and socially from your present and future. It can permit doubt to overtake hope and to cause defeat to replace success. In times when fear appears to have not just been passing by, and it visits for a period longer than you would expect, find faith. Faith has the ability to transform fear into a positive emotion. Faith can restore in all areas of your well-being. Faith has the power to make you a victor and not a victim. Try faith.

Writing/Journal/Action/Discussion/Reflection Prompt:

What does fear mean to you? What does faith mean to you? How and why have you allowed one emotion to overpower the other emotion? Please be specific. Lastly, how can you allow fear to exist but not to hamper the processes of life?

Day 111

I'm a limited edition.

You are uniquely and unequivocally you. There are people who share the same talents, interests, characteristics, ideals, race, gender, age, education, and more as you, but you still have the combination unlike any other. You have different thoughts, ideals, values, beliefs, practices and more. The way you do that certain thing differs slightly from another. Simply put, there exists no one exactly like you.

Writing/Journal/Action/Discussion/Reflection Prompt:

Identify one way extrinsically and one way intrinsically that you differ from other individuals who might be compared to you?

Day 112

Be you not them.

Permit this to be your mantra at all times, especially when the pressures of trying to fit-in or emulate someone else enters your mind and/or guides your actions.

Writing/Journal/Action/Discussion/Reflection Prompt:

What is one way that you have tried to be someone else? Discuss with someone why is being you difficult in your environment.

Day 113

Do what you love, and do it often.

The more you do the things that bring you joy and fulfillment the more positivity you release into your life and the world.

Writing/Journal/Action/Discussion/Reflection Prompt:

What is one thing that you love doing? How can you do this more frequently? Tomorrow is a great opportunity to do it.

Day 114

Time to get stuff done!

Why are delaying for another day, week, month, or year? The best time to do it is now and not in the near or far-off future. Possibly, you have not thought through the process, devised a plan, or gathered all of the necessary components. Nevertheless, this should not delay some level of preparation or action on your part. You must realize that if you do not it will not be done.

Writing/Journal/Action/Discussion/Reflection Prompt:

What is something that you have put-off far too long? What is the primary reason for your delaying? In what way(s) can you begin preparing today?

Day 115

Dreams do come true!

You might be thinking that is what happens if wishes and shooting stars are factors; someone is famous; or this is part of a plot in a book, a movie, or a television show. You might even believe that this is possible for others just not you. Fortunately, neither of the aforementioned are the only absolutes. Your dreams can come true, but you must have faith that what you imagine is possible for you. Imagining must become effort, which involves hard work, commitment, mistakes, re-dos, doubt, and belief. Soon, you realize that you are closer to accomplishing what was once a dream. Eventually, your dream is your reality.

Writing/Journal/Action/Discussion/Reflection Prompt:

Do you believe that dreams come true for all people? Who are the people for whom dreams do not (or easily) come true? Explain your response.

Day 116

Radiate positivity.

The opposite is unimaginable.

Writing/Journal/Action/Discussion/Reflection Prompt:

Are you an individual who radiates positivity? Why or why not?

Day 117

Choose your own path.

Have you ever gone on a walk or a hike in an unfamiliar area? Have you ever made a decision that you were uncertain as to the outcome? Have you ever followed the beckoning or urgings of another even when you knew that this was not the best choice? Have you ever taken steps that would cause the least amount of frustration, disappointment, or pain only to arrive at an unsatisfactory outcome? Have you ever literally walked in someone else's footsteps? Your responses to these five questions suggest whether you are a leader or a follower. There will be times when either descriptor is appropriate. There will be times when one descriptor is more suitable than the other descriptor. What is most important is that you take the path that is beneficial for you at that moment, whether in the lead, following behind, or on your own.

Writing/Journal/Action/Discussion/Reflection Prompt:

Are you predominantly a leader, follower, or loner? What is a critical factor in your choice of descriptor?

Day 118

Let the world hear you roar!

Lions roar. Whether a cub or adult and male or female, lions have powerful roars that can be heard at a distance. Humans speak. Whether a male or female child, adolescent, or adult, humans have powerful voices that can be heard at a distance. Lions use their roars in the same manner that humans use their voice—to communicate with those of like kind. When a lion wants to communicate with another lion, it roars. When a human wants to communicate with another human, they speak. For lions and humans, the intensity of the sound projected is dependent upon the severity of the message to be received. You probably are thinking, "What does a lion have to do with me?" Well, directly, not much but indirectly, there is some correlation. Lions are endowed with the ability to exert power through their voice. You are endowed with the ability to exert your power through your voice. Consequently, the next time that you have something to say that must be conveyed, can improve the status quo, is often ignored, or believe that you do not possess the level of power needed to get others to listen, channel your inner lion and roar. Your message will undeniably be heard.

Writing/Journal/Action/Discussion/Reflection Prompt:

What is something that someone living or deceased has said that resonated with you? Why did their message impact you in that manner?

Day 119

Be yourself. Everyone else is already taken.

I know that you have heard or read someone express in one way or another that being an original is the best option for anyone. Well, this is the truth that you should live every day of your life. If you elect the alternative, you would be living a lie.

Writing/Journal/Action/Discussion/Reflection Prompt:

Who is someone that if you could switch places with you would? What does/did this person represent that you believe to be of significance for yourself?

Day 120

Positive vibes only.

You attract what you emit. If you want to exist in positive spaces and interact with positive people, the only option is for you to be positive. When negativity emerges, resist it with positivity.

Writing/Journal/Action/Discussion/Reflection Prompt:

Who is the most positive person that you know? Does their positivity affect you?

Day 121

"May your choices follow your hopes not your fears."
– Nelson Mandela

Every decision that you make in life should be one rooted in reflection, conviction, and probability. Thinking before acting is essential in all matters, whether significant or trivial. Principles should guide your options, whether easy or difficult. Possibilities should be the compelling force as you navigate away from your doubts. Do not experience life dictated by anxieties. Experience life governed by positive-based potentials.

Writing/Journal/Action/Discussion/Reflection Prompt:

Identify one fear that can work on removing from your life in the next couple of weeks.

Day 122

(Get it done!)

You are the most important factor in making happen for yourself what you want to happen. If you neither begin nor complete the task, you will not prepare for what will follow. Stop delaying! Start doing!

Writing/Journal/Action/Discussion/Reflection Prompt:

What is something that you need to begin and/or complete this or next week? List two steps that you must take to make it happen.

Day 123

Color outside the lines.

Do you consider yourself a divergent thinker or doer? Are you an individual who chooses to take the alternate route more often than not in life? Do you think that the status quo should not be static? Do you offer atypical responses more frequently than common ones? If so, you approach life on your own terms, at least most of the time. When you believe that something is not as it should be, you make it known to others. You are an individual and have the right to display your individuality in its entire splendor, just as long as you are not being offensive, infringing upon the rights of others, or violating a law. Your insight supports those who stay within the lines to expand their thinking, personally grow, and strengthen their resolve.

Writing/Journal/Action/Discussion/Reflection Prompt:

When did you first begin to "color" the world within your own perimeters? Explain in detail what prompted you and how you do this in your life.

Day 124

(Live to inspire.)

Your placement on this earth is for more than your benefit. Your purpose has a connection to others—near and far. It is certain that sometimes, your influence will be neither intentional nor known by you. Try to leave an impression that is unquestionable and meaningful to others. Always, live as if others are watching. By doing so, you encourage others.

Writing/Journal/Action/Discussion/Reflection Prompt:

In what ways do you believe that you inspire others? What is one way that you can intentionally inspire others moving forward?

Day 125

Choose happiness.

No other possibility should exist for you. Life will bring moments and periods of despair, hopelessness, and uncertainty. Even during those times, find something about your day and/or your life for which you can be thankful. Through moments of joy, you suppress the opposite emotions.

Writing/Journal/Action/Discussion/Reflection Prompt:

Why do you sometimes allow feelings that are oppose happiness to control your emotions? Identify one specific way that you can combat this occurrence in the future.

Day 126

This girl can! This boy can!

Regardless of your gender, if you try with all possible might, you can achieve what you desire! Society prescribes certain perimeters for females and males. However, you do not have to accommodate those boundaries. Become that person who you want to be in life. In fact, do it to the level that even surpasses expectations.

Writing/Journal/Action/Discussion/Reflection Prompt:

What is a profession that you want to pursue? To what gender does society associate this profession? What or who propels you forward to defy the limits of society?

Day 127

If you never try it, you'll never know.

Do not base your conclusions off someone else's experience. You must realize that you and everyone else have innate strengths, weaknesses, talents, and inabilities. Yet in still, you should not let people or things inhibit you from endeavoring new and unexpected possibilities. The best outcome is to try and then succeed. The second best outcome is to try and then fail. The worst outcome is never to try at all.

Writing/Journal/Action/Discussion/Reflection Prompt:

What are you fearful to try? What or who is influencing you to remain fearful? Discuss one significant strategy that you will use so that you can move forward and try.

Day 128

Don't give up until you are proud.

Sometimes, you stop before reaching the point that you deem satisfactory. Possibly, you stop sooner than expected because of your own fear or negative thoughts. Possibly, you do not continue because of someone else's opinions or doubts. You might do things in life to appease or satisfy other's wants and needs. Do not do this. You should be the inspiration for beginning, carrying-out, and reaching your goal(s). Your satisfaction should be the guarantee in determining the end in anything that you do for yourself.

Writing/Journal/Action/Discussion/Reflection Prompt:

What is something that you have given-up on before you reached your desired goal? Strongly consider trying again.

Day 129

My favorite blessing is my ___.

You fill-in the blank. With a grateful heart, boldly walk through each day.

Writing/Journal/Action/Discussion/Reflection Prompt:

With what word did you fill-in the blank? How will you demonstrate that this person, place, thing, or idea is significant to you?

Day 130

be still.

Listening and silence are essential for progress. Choosing to wait rather than to act or speak often leads to desired outcomes. Being compelled to respond is not an indicator that a reaction or response is necessary. Take some time to reflect upon the situation. The result(s) conceivably will be more worthwhile than you expect.

Writing/Journal/Action/Discussion/Reflection Prompt:

Why is it difficult to wait? How can silence be beneficial in your life?

Day 131

Do more of what makes you happy.

You deserve to live a fulfilling and contented life. Relying upon others to bring those components into your life is unproductive thinking and flawed action or lack thereof. Doing what brings you enjoyment includes developing your character and identity. You have the majority of the control in those areas. Do not place that responsibility on anyone else.

Writing/Journal/Action/Discussion/Reflection Prompt:

What is something that you can do to make your life happier? Begin doing it as soon as possible.

Day 132

Today is a good day.

No matter what lies ahead as you embark upon each day, remember that you are the regulator of your thoughts. Do not permit anyone's perspective to influence your viewpoint negatively.

Writing/Journal/Action/Discussion/Reflection Prompt:

What is one way that you maintain a positive perspective?

Day 133

Give thanks.

In all situations and for all things, be gracious. Be mindful that a grateful stance opens many doors; while, an ungrateful stance closes many doors.

Writing/Journal/Action/Discussion/Reflection Prompt:

What is one way that you give thanks?

Day 134

Life is all about balance.

To the extent of an aerialist on a trapeze or tightrope, awareness of one's next move is most favorable. The slightest movement can disturb the equilibrium in all scenarios. As in life, you will experience certainties and uncertainties. However, the decision that you make when life becomes unsteady is just as critical when life is stable. Proceed with your eyes upon your target and prepare yourself for expected and unexpected obstacles along the way.

Writing/Journal/Action/Discussion/Reflection Prompt:

What advice do you have for someone who cannot find balance in life? If you do not have advice, who is someone that you can seek advice from on this matter?

Day 135

Be unique.

Express yourself with diversity, individuality, originality, and personality. Give 100% of every aspect that makes you distinctively you.

Writing/Journal/Action/Discussion/Reflection Prompt:

Would others consider you unique or common? Why or why not?

Day 136

Sunny days would not be special if there wasn't rain.

Positivity counteracts negativity. Success counteracts disappointment. Hope counteracts fear. Satisfaction counteracts disappointment. You must encounter the opposite of pleasing experiences in order to truly value the beauty of life.

Writing/Journal/Action/Discussion/Reflection Prompt:

What does the statement for today mean to you? Provide deeper insight in your response.

Day 137

Cupcakes are muffins that believed in miracles.

When you begin life's journey, you do not have a roadmap to follow in the direction of your destiny. Rather, you take steps forward. As you progress, expect that what is good, beautiful, and purposeful will meet you along the way. Rely on the knowledge that bad situations and things can result in good situations and things; displeasing people and circumstances can become beautiful people and circumstances; and indecision can lead to purpose. When in doubt, think of (or eat a) the cupcake.

Writing/Journal/Action/Discussion/Reflection Prompt:

What is another metaphor that parallels the cupcake and the muffin? Now, envision how you will be the victor the next time that you need a miracle?

Day 138

Let go and let faith!

Stop trying to control everyone and everything that happens in and around your life. You were not created to solve every situation or problem that involves and does not involve you. Even if you can help, you cannot do it all. Allow belief in the Creator to help you decrease your level of input and involvement and observe your faith increase exponentially.

Writing/Journal/Action/Discussion/Reflection Prompt:

What is something that you agree is too big for you to solve? Give faith a chance in that situation.

Day 139

Live like the gate was left open.

Boundaries at times are necessary to keep you safe. However, on other occasions, boundaries can limit you from excelling to the highest of heights. It is imperative that you learn how to discern when to remain within and when to push margins. Allow your principles, intellect, and conscience to guide you up to, into, and beyond the gates in your life.

Writing/Journal/Action/Discussion/Reflection Prompt:

What is one boundary that has limited you from excelling in an area of your life? How can you mindfully use that boundary to propel you towards the level that you choose?

Day 140

Roll with it!

It is alright if people identify you as "cautious." Choosing to weigh your options before entering into or doing something is a sign of wisdom. However, there will be times when it is adequate to be spontaneous, to go against the grain, or allow someone else to be in charge. Relax. What is the worst thing that could happen? You enjoy yourself!?

Writing/Journal/Action/Discussion/Reflection Prompt:

What is one area of your life that you are hesitant to let go of the reigns because you fear losing control of the situation? How can you begin to be less cautious?

Day 141

Bloom where you are planted.

One significant thing plants do not have is the ability to uproot themselves, find a new environment, become rooted, and continue to grow. You on the other-hand do have the ability to transplant yourself and find new environments in which to grow. Simply possessing this ability does not foster the necessity to do so. Where you presently are in life might not be where you want to be in life but that does not mean that you are in a completely stagnant or stifling environment. Just like plants, you have the ability to thrive in the harshest conditions and settings. Rather than uproot yourself and possibly the lives of others, allow your roots to survive, grow deeper into the soil, receive nutrients, and flourish in the present environment.

Writing/Journal/Action/Discussion/Reflection Prompt:

Do you believe that your present environment is repressive or liberating? Provide details to support your response.

Day 142

Rise up and pray.

Begin your day in prayer. Express gratitude for life and the opportunities that lie ahead for you. Continue the day with anticipation that you will witness your hopes become reality. Tomorrow, repeat the process.

Writing/Journal/Action/Discussion/Reflection Prompt:

What is one thing that you release in prayer?

Day 143

Focus on the good.

Why focus on the negative?

Writing/Journal/Action/Discussion/Reflection Prompt:

What are two good people, places, things, and concepts that you give your attention? List them and consciously focus on them.

Day 144

Smart is the new vibe.

Everyone is smart. Everyone has intelligence(s). Put your smarts on display. Not only will you be the better for doing so but also will the world.

Writing/Journal/Action/Discussion/Reflection Prompt:

Research the eight intelligences identified by Howard Gardner in 1983. Which intelligence do you believe describes you the best? Why?

Day 145

I'm too fabulous to fit in.

Stand out! Stand up! Be bold! Be brave! Be seen! Be heard! Get noticed! Accept that you are not like everyone else.

Writing/Journal/Action/Discussion/Reflection Prompt:

What makes you different from others? Is it an intrinsic or extrinsic characteristic?

Day 146

"That which does not kill us makes us stronger." – Friedrich Nietzsche

You will encounter hardships, setbacks, and seemingly unsurmountable odds in life. Do not give in to defeat. Persist until difficulty becomes triumph, and you have a testament that the situation was not the end of a purpose but a purpose with an end. You survived, and you are stronger.

Writing/Journal/Action/Discussion/Reflection Prompt:

What is one situation that you believed that you would not endure? How did this situation strengthen your resolve?

Day 147

Always have hope.

Tomorrow is a new day for new opportunities and new outcomes.

Writing/Journal/Action/Discussion/Reflection Prompt:

Why is it important to remain hopeful during difficult situations? Find someone who is in need hope and encourage them.

Day 148

Weird is a side effect of being.

The longer that you spend time on Earth, the more time that you have at becoming you. Unusual, odd, uncanny, and strange are merely words that describe nouns. Do not allow people, including yourself, to use these or similar adjectives in a negative manner to define you.

Writing/Journal/Action/Discussion/Reflection Prompt:

Identify one manner in which others or you would describe yourself as "weird"? Remember, this description does not define you.

Day 149

"Don't put the key to your happiness in someone else's pocket." – Swami Chinmayananda

You should never give someone else permission to hold your joy or control your contentment. You should be the sole possessor of your sources of well-being. One simple reason is that when you need access, access might not be granted to you.

Writing/Journal/Action/Discussion/Reflection Prompt:

Do you rely upon others to bring happiness into your life? Why or why not?

Day 150

Take your dreams seriously.

Your dreams are not capable of taking you seriously.

Writing/Journal/Action/Discussion/Reflection Prompt:

Identify one dream that you do not take seriously because of the opinion(s) of others. Who are the people who are holding you back from pursuing this dream? Think of you strategy to implement to get these people to believe in your dream.

Day 151

Believe in miracles.

Miracles cannot be unfortunate happenings. Miracles are quite often unexpected but hoped for occurrences. When you place your faith in the unseen, unimaginable, and even impossible (thing to happen), you have the belief for a miracle. If you are directly or indirectly in a situation that is dependent upon a miracle, believe! Miracles do happen.

Writing/Journal/Action/Discussion/Reflection Prompt:

Discuss a time that someone close to you or you experienced a miracle. How did the miracle change their or your life for the better?

Day 152

Every day love, smile, hope, learn, share, hug, be happy, and be kind.

These are the essentials of life. Consider these as vitamins—L1, S1, H1, L1, S2, H2, H3, and K1. They do not exist in a multi-vitamin form. If you want to develop into the person that you have the potential to become in life, it is necessary that you demonstrate and/or experience each of these essentials daily. They will help you maintain balance in life and promote a positive perspective.

Writing/Journal/Action/Discussion/Reflection Prompt:

Which of the eight essentials do you get sufficient amounts daily in your life? Which of the eight essentials do you need more daily in your life?

Day 153

Work hard. Dream big.

Significant dreams require initiative and determination. If you are not willing to put in the required level of input, you will not obtain the desired level output. When you have substantial hopes, be prepared to invest substantial time and effort to accomplish them.

Writing/Journal/Action/Discussion/Reflection Prompt:

Have you ever wanted something to happen but were not willing to invest in the desired outcome? Why or why not?

Day 154

Life is a journey. Trust the ride.

Your life is like a roadmap with both expected and unexpected stops along the way. As you transition from one stop to the next, you might get off-course or experience delays in reaching your destination. These are not signs that you will not arrive at your intended destination, but these can be signs that what you expect might not happen exactly as you foresee in life. Whatever preferred mode of transportation, take all the necessary precautions and enjoy the journey. You will eventually reach the point of destination.

Writing/Journal/Action/Discussion/Reflection Prompt:

Where do you want to be by end of the current year? What do you want to accomplish by December 31st?

Day 155

"Keep an eye on the stars and feet on the ground."
Theodore Roosevelt

No one should discourage you from having magnanimous dreams. However, any hope that you possess should be rooted in and guided by reality. Many people use the constellations to guide them in reaching their goal. All the same, while one eye's focus is on a shining collection of gaseous substances, your other eye must concentrate on the Earthly possibilities as you purposefully walk unto your future.

Writing/Journal/Action/Discussion/Reflection Prompt:

Why do people tell other's that their goal(s) is unrealistic?

Day 156

Throw kindness around like confetti.

Shower people with love, generosity, and goodwill. These types of precipitation neither harm the natural environment nor humankind.

Writing/Journal/Action/Discussion/Reflection Prompt:

Would you be appreciative or resentful if someone showed you a considerable amount of benevolence? Support your response with an example, personal or fiction.

Day 157

"All the flowers of all the tomorrows are in the seeds of today." – Native American Proverb

Inspiration is fleeting. When inspiration comes to you, do not bottle it, and place it on a shelf for another time. Take hold of it, cultivate it, and share it with the world.

Writing/Journal/Action/Discussion/Reflection Prompt:

What does the "flower" in the proverb stand for to you? Why?

Day 158

There is always something to be thankful for.

Whether a smile upon an unfamiliar person's face, a ray of sunshine breaking through a cluster of clouds in the sky, another opportunity to say, "I love you," a shooting star in the darkest of night, or the dawning of a new day, you have so many reasons for which to give thanks. Each day, pick one.

Writing/Journal/Action/Discussion/Reflection Prompt:

What is something that you are thankful for that others might dismiss or ignore?

Day 159

The grass is always greener where you water it.

Those things, ideas, places, and people that matter most deserve your attention. If either of these areas are lacking in anyway, take the time to nourish them. You might be amazed at the effect of your interest.

Writing/Journal/Action/Discussion/Reflection Prompt:

What have you neglected lately? Why?

Day 160

Cool kid [person] just showed up.

You are amazing, regardless of what people say or believe. Embrace all aspects of who you are and represent. If there is something that you feel needs improvement or you are not fond of about yourself, change it. If it is something that someone else perceives, deeply consider the merits of the suggestion and make the best decision for and about yourself.

Writing/Journal/Action/Discussion/Reflection Prompt:

Do you believe that you are a cool kid? Why or why not? Do others believe that you are a cool kid? Why or why not?

Day 161

I love you to the moon and back.

Your love for others is variable. For some, it is deep in both feeling and expression. For others, it exists on a surface level. For others, it is insignificantly shared or absent. Today's statement is reflective of love that transcends boundaries and includes expressions that do not require intense affection. Try showing some level of love toward everyone moving forward.

Writing/Journal/Action/Discussion/Reflection Prompt:

How do you know when you are loved? How do you know that you love someone or something?

Day 162

Never stop dreaming.

The only time that dreaming ceases is when your soul is absent from your body. Until then, keep believing, expecting, and progressing towards your aspirations.

Writing/Journal/Action/Discussion/Reflection Prompt:

Why do people stop dreaming? Have you ever stopped dreaming? Why or why not?

Day 163

Focus on the good.

Attention given to negativity is not only detrimental to your physical well-being but also your mental well-being. Negative images bombard your mind daily, whether directly or indirectly. Do not allow someone's or your own harmful actions, thoughts, words, perspectives, and beliefs to slant what you know to be truth. If or when given the opportunity, encourage and redirect others to the truth.

Writing/Journal/Action/Discussion/Reflection Prompt:

What is one aspect of life or one area in which you can find positivity, especially one in which negativity appears to have more significance? How can/will you diminish the negative in order to increase the positive?

Day 164

"The best preparation for tomorrow is doing your best today." – H. Jackson Brown, Jr.

If you want your tomorrow to be better than your today, you have to be proactive. Proactivity means acknowledging and taking ownership of the possibilities that lie ahead, whether foreseen or unforeseen. Proactivity entails rectifying mistakes, planning your next steps, and accomplishing tasks. Proactivity wins over reactivity every time.

Writing/Journal/Action/Discussion/Reflection Prompt:

What is something in the near future that you should begin preparing for now?

Day 165

Stay fierce.

You are powerful. Within you lies the intensity to inspire, impact, affect positive change in your immediate and distant environment. Use your ferocity for good not evil, to build and not destroy, to expand not diminish. If someone counters your initiative, stay true. If someone aligns with your cause, join forces. In all situations, remain strong.

Writing/Journal/Action/Discussion/Reflection Prompt:

Do you consider yourself to be strong or weak overall? Why?

Day 166

"There is no elevator to success; you must take the stairs." – Zig Ziglar

Do you want fame and fortune? Do you want it as fast as possible? Sure there are immediate routes, but they do not always lead you to your anticipated destination. Taking the more involved route offers new perspectives and opportunities as well as trials and errors. These factors make your success more meaningful and memorable.

Writing/Journal/Action/Discussion/Reflection Prompt:

Would you rather have a fast or slow means to success? Provide a detailed reason and include what type of success?

Day 168

Don't quit.

Giving-up and giving-in is often easier than standing firm and resisting the impulse. What you are experiencing might be challenging and even appear unsurmountable; nevertheless, dismiss the destructive persuasion(s). Persevere and wait for the encouragements that will guide you to the finish.

Writing/Journal/Action/Discussion/Reflection Prompt:

Have you ever quit something? Why or why not? Do you have any regrets for quitting or not quitting?

Day 167

This is the day we change the world.

Are you filled with anticipation? Are you seeking a purpose greater than what you see, know, or live? Are you inspired to make the world the best it has ever been in history? Are you unafraid of being told, "No?" Are you willing to go the distance? Are you ready to join hands with friends and strangers of all races, ethnicities, cultures, ages, gender, foreign, domestic? Are you ready?

Writing/Journal/Action/Discussion/Reflection Prompt:

Name one way in which you want to improve the world, include why?

Day 169

Every day is a second chance.

Have you ever awakened on a new day and thought, "If I could only relive that moment or yesterday?" If so, you are not alone. Every person older than five-years of age experiences or senses regret throughout their life because of something that they did or did not say or do. Sometimes, you will not be able to rectify or erase something from the past regardless of the amount of effort that you put into the situation. Neither fear nor have self-pity, the fact that you feel compelled is a positive sign. Take notice of this, and do whatever is within your control to do better, try again, so that the next time, you have no regrets.

Writing/Journal/Action/Discussion/Reflection Prompt:

Are second chances a guarantee? Why or why not?

Day 170

Write. Read.

Writing is the expression of complete thoughts into intelligible sentences with a subject and a verb that adhere to standard forms of spelling, grammar, punctuation, and structure. Reading is the undertaking of comprehending visual (or tactile) characters in the form of letters that signify meaning, denotatively and connotatively. Both of these words reflect action. Both of these words are vital functions of everyday living. With everything within you, exercise both of these actions in order to communicate, connect, and transfer with humanity.

Writing/Journal/Action/Discussion/Reflection Prompt:

Which of the two actions, write and read, do you prefer the most? Why? Provide specific details to support your preference.

Day 171

You make a difference in the world.

Your presence in the world is like no other. No other being has the exact make-up as you. Your talents, skills, and beliefs help make you unique. What you want to say, what you want to do, and how you want to contribute to society is both needed and wanted even if you do not know that today. Find your chosen way to give physically, mentally, and/or spiritually to the world, now!

Writing/Journal/Action/Discussion/Reflection Prompt:

What is one significant way that you would like to have influence in the world in the present or near future? Discuss your response in detail.

Day 172

"If I cannot do great things, I can do small things in a great way." – Dr. Martin Luther King Jr.

Dr. Martin Luther King, Jr. was a man who had a vision. Some viewed his foresight as other-worldly, magnanimous, and even awe inspiring. Regardless of your perspective of the man, his mission was undeniable. He wanted to promote (agape) love and kindness, equitable opportunities and treatment, and universal understanding and acceptance for/towards all humankind. Charged with his personal mission and the support of those with a common goal, he took steps that led him down a path to combat oppressive systems and promote social justice reform.

Writing/Journal/Action/Discussion/Reflection Prompt:

Identify someone past or present who exemplified Dr. King's statement, include how they did as well.

Day 173

Prove them wrong!

In life, you will encounter those individuals deemed as pessimists, doubters, and "haters."

These persons rarely acknowledge (publicly) their own fears and envies and refuse to believe the best for you in most if not all situations. They can become very vocal with the spreading of their negative perspective, whether based upon evidence or not. Rather than retaliate or respond with matched sentiment, show them that they are incorrect in their assessment of your abilities, skills, and you. Do not spend too much time trying to represent the contrary to their belief. Merely live your life with the assuredness that the perception(s) that others hold of you that do not align with your own perception(s) of self cannot hold you back from achieving and living your truth.

Writing/Journal/Action/Discussion/Reflection Prompt:

Have you ever proved the perception of someone wrong as it applies to you? If so, how did you do it, and who held this viewpoint? If you have never, discuss someone else or another group of people that have.

Day 174

(Stand up; speak out!)

You are a living being who has both shared and uncommonly held beliefs, values, experiences, truths, and knowledge about the world and all aspects associated with it, including other living beings. By virtue, you are entitled to share your feelings, viewpoints, and thoughts about any one or more of those aspects within the purview of the law. Consequently, if you see injustice, stand up; speak out! If you disagree with a practice or system, sand up; speak out! If you want to see transformative change, stand up; speak out! If you want to be heard, stand up; speak out! Do not hold back. Stand up; speak out! You will neither be the first nor the last person in history to do so.

Writing/Journal/Action/Discussion/Reflection Prompt:

Discuss a time when you chose to not standup and/or speak out about something that you did not agree. Discuss a time when you when you chose to standup and/or speak out about something that you did not agree. Include the situation or issue and the why in your responses.

Day 175

Believe there is good in the world.

For most people, evil is the opposite of good. The presence of evil is not a definitive that goodness does not exist. Specifically, the presence of goodness is overshadowed by evil. People, things, ideas, and places can be associated with this term. From current observation, evil appears to be prevalent in all areas within society. Nevertheless, the application of good can defeat incarnations of evil. Believe good exists. Seek goodness even when it appears as if evil is dominant. Evil does not have to prevail.

Writing/Journal/Action/Discussion/Reflection Prompt:

From your perspective, what is an area of existence that you believe lacks goodness and share why you believe this.

Day 176

Make things happen!

What are you waiting on? If you identify a need, have an agenda, see a void, or develop an urge, put in action what needs to be done. If you cannot do it alone, seek the aid of others. We are waiting on (them and) you!

Writing/Journal/Action/Discussion/Reflection Prompt:

What is something that you are waiting to happen? Why have you not started?

Day 177

"Enjoy the little things in life, for some day you will realize they were the big things." – Kurt Vonnegut, Jr.

What you deem as menial today just might have mammoth influence in your life's experience in retrospect. Rather than diminish the events that you directly or indirectly experience, find value in every moment. You certainly do not want to live life through recollections.

Writing/Journal/Action/Discussion/Reflection Prompt:

What is an event or occurrence that you did not realize the significance until much later? How can you lessen this happening in your life moving forward?

Day 178

Do what is right not what is easy.

Morality and ethics are aspects of life that you begin to form in your childhood. Family, friends, acquaintances, religion, government, educational institutions, society, and life experiences are significant influencers as well as the media, Internet, and social platforms. Each of these influencers can guide you in direct and indirect ways towards positive and negative outcomes. In life, it is only expected that these influences will play vital roles in shaping your thoughts, judgements, and beliefs about the people, places, things, ideas, and actions that you encounter on a daily basis. Try not to get overwhelmed. Treat each opportunity independently of other opportunities when applying principles. Take circumstances into account and put prejudgments to the side. The goal in life is to do what you consider morally and ethically right despite the time and labor involved in the decision-making process.

Writing/Journal/Action/Discussion/Reflection Prompt:

Identify a time when you believe someone, or you did not base a decision upon what society identifies as right or wrong. How could this decision have been more meaningful if societal norms been a factor? Provide details. Do not share anything that you believe to be too personal or private.

Day 179

I love being awesome!

Whether others or you consider yourself remarkable, amazing, fearsome, and/or splendid, embrace these adjectives. In the most humane and least presumptuous manner, put your awesomeness on display for all to experience.

Writing/Journal/Action/Discussion/Reflection Prompt:

What is one way that you are impressive? If you do not believe this about yourself, identify one way that you can be impressive in a non-overconfident way?

Day 180

Life is good!

Is it not? If it is not, find a means to make it better. Whether in a grand or humble way, create the life that you want and offers you the opportunities to bring light into the world.

Writing/Journal/Action/Discussion/Reflection Prompt:

What is something that you can do today as a starting point to bring (more) joy into your life?

Day 181

Believe [...]

in the impossible.
in the unknown.
that wonderful things will happen for you.
that in your tomorrow awaits infinite possibilities.
that you have a purpose.
you can manage your most seemingly demanding situations.
the direction in which you are going is divinely orchestrated.
mistakes are opportunity for growth.
there is meaning to everything that happens in life.

Writing/Journal/Action/Discussion/Reflection Prompt:

Take one of the statements and expound upon that thought. Make direct connection to your present or hoped for life.

Day 182

"Self-confidence is the best outfit. Rock it. Own it."

Self-confidence does not have to be rooted in conceit. It does not have to remain in your closet, and you only wear it on special occasions. Sometimes, others might perceive that it is too small or large, does not fit your "type", out of or in-style. Whatever might be the attitude, remember, you have your own sense of style/confidence, which is continually evolving and adapting to your wants and needs not theirs. You never know, your style just might influence someone else.

Writing/Journal/Action/Discussion/Reflection Prompt:

Are you self-confident? Why or why not? What is one area in which you could gain or grow stronger in confidence?

Day 183

Take the one less traveled.

Pathway. Road. Flight. Voyage. Journey. Adventure.

Writing/Journal/Action/Discussion/Reflection Prompt:

Which of the six options appeals to you most? Why?

Day 184

Off you go to change the world.

You made it. You have reached that milestone. You have a great foundation upon which to build and make your mark in society. Do not focus on the how, when, what, or where. Simply live a life rooted in human kindness and love.

Writing/Journal/Action/Discussion/Reflection Prompt:

What is a milestone that you will reach soon? What is next? Explain in detail your post-milestone plans.

Day 185

Love your life!

If you are not capable, find what is at the source. Find time to reflect and be introspective. Take the necessary actions and step towards change. This is necessary to love your life.

Writing/Journal/Action/Discussion/Reflection Prompt:

What do you love most about your life? Why?

Day 186

Do one thing every day that makes you happy.

Whether in nature, with people or animals, at your favorite location, or alone, carpe diem and create a moment of blessedness. From sitting in silence to protesting for change amongst a crowd of thousands, from reading a book in café to standing on a stage sharing a talent with the world, from finding solace in nature to viewing the human landscape as you travel the world, experience everyday self-approval.

Writing/Journal/Action/Discussion/Reflection Prompt:

If you could do one thing each day, what would it be, and why is this the thing?

Day 187

To travel is to live.

Near or far, stateside or abroad, around the corner and back, by foot or plane, from earth to outer space, imagined or real-time, take journeys in life. The experience might just change your life.

Writing/Journal/Action/Discussion/Reflection Prompt:

What is your most desired travel destination? Why?

Day 188

You are braver than you know, stronger than you seem, smarter than you think, and loved more than you know.

What! You did not know this about yourself? Let me be the first person to tell you. During 2020 and 2021, you have survived a global pandemic, witnessed/participated in national and global outcries against social injustice, faced (and overcome) personal challenges/setbacks, realized aspects about yourself that you were not aware, and awakened to new levels of self-determination.

Writing/Journal/Action/Discussion/Reflection Prompt:

What is something positive that you realized about yourself during the past year or a negative situation?

Day 189

(Failure can be the first steps toward success.)

It is inevitable. You will experience matters that do not conclude with the expected outcome and can simply be identified as disappointments, letdowns, and flops. In those instances, do not react as many often do and lose all faith or quit in achieving your aspired result. Instead, in that moment (or some days following), identify—positive facet(s) of the experience or situation, areas in which you can improve, and necessary steps to move forward. In time, you will find that you are looking back at those former times as moments of preparation for achievement. Remember, valuable lessons are learned from victories as well as defeats.

Writing/Journal/Action/Discussion/Reflection Prompt:

What is one valuable lesson that you learned from a negative experience or outcome that you can share with and be beneficial to someone?

Day 190

"Tough times don't last tough people do." – Robert H. Schuller

Have you ever thought, "How did they survive that situation; why have they never given-up; or what continues to inspire them despite their lived circumstances"? These and many more questions are common. It is inevitable that every human being, including you, will encounter hardships, difficult times, setbacks, mishaps, and even defeats. It is also certain that with the passage of time that negative, unexpected, uncomfortable, or unfortunate encounters will transition into better and even positive encounters. Nevertheless, what is most important during those times is how you (humans) respond to/in those situations. The key is to not give-up or give-in to the adverse experience. Rather, the goal is to persist through the experience; learn more about others, your environment, things, and yourself; and maintain a constructive attitude and perspective about the outcome regardless of what others and you say, believe, and do during the situation. Look beyond the present circumstances and envision the conclusion you want. Before you realize it, you have overcome whatever was plaguing you. The next time or situation, your fortitude will progress you through once again.

Writing/Journal/Action/Discussion/Reflection Prompt:

Who is someone that you truly believe is representative of today's quotation? Explain why you identified this person and how they embody the passage.

Day 191

"[H]ope [is] an anchor for the soul." – Hebrews 6: 19

Faith is the foundation of hope. In life, you want certain things to happen in your favor, seek assurances along the journey that your experiences will result in positive consequences, and affirm what aligns with your aspirations. However, in order for you to confidently (as possible) keep moving in the right trajectory, you must possess a degree of expectation that is greater than the degrees of impossibility. Otherwise, your efforts are bound to disappoint you if no one else. Each day, find a Higher Power both within and outside yourself and root your dreams, goals, and undertakings in at as you forge to do and/or see both the possible and the impossible happen in your life.

Writing/Journal/Action/Discussion/Reflection Prompt:

Are you a person who has or lacks hope? Why?

Day 192

"Education is the most powerful weapon which you can use to change the world." – Nelson Mandela

Education is power, or some similar statement has been uttered by the famous, infamous, and unknown. Education is the key to unlock knowledge and tap into undiscovered potential. One such potential being effective change. If you want to stimulate positive and lasting transformation within society—social, political, environmental, or other systems, if you want to change the way that humanity interacts and utilizes the natural world—all plant life, animal life, celestial formations, land, water, air, if you want to sustain the good things while improving the bad, (a) you must educate yourself; (b) you must find like-minded and like willed individuals; (c) you must devise a methodical approach; (d) you must take action and remain steadfast despite the opposition; and (e) empower yourself and others. If you do not feel sufficiently equipped, seek resources—people, ideas, and things that can assist and provide guidance. Do not devalue the power of your education.

Writing/Journal/Action/Discussion/Reflection Prompt:

How powerful has your education been for you? Describe at least one way that your education could empower you to be a change agent in society. Find another person who shares a similar viewpoint and collectively begin the process.

Day 193

(You hold the key to your happiness.)

What lies behind the door, gate, or portal awaits you. You can give your key to someone else, but they cannot truly identify for you what is happiness. You can lose your key, but you are the only one who can find it again. The only way that you can experience it is to seek and find it for yourself. Why are you waiting? Take the key and unlock it—happiness, contentment, delight, and joy.

Writing/Journal/Action/Discussion/Reflection Prompt:

Discuss a time when you were not be happy. How did or what caused you to be happy?

Day 194

Your vibe attracts your tribe.

Your energy, signals, messages, and professions, whether verbally or non-verbally communicated, draws like energy, signals, messages, and professions towards you. Unlike magnets, you do not repel people who are like you. Rather, you draw them towards you. If you want to surround yourself with love, positivity, and light, you must radiate love, positivity, and light. Releasing hate, negativity, and darkness into the universe will never bring the opposite. If it does, beware! Ultimately, whatever you want in life, you must give in life.

Writing/Journal/Action/Discussion/Reflection Prompt:

How has this statement been affirmed in your lifetime, personally or non-personally?

Day 195

(You don't make mistakes. Mistakes make you, if you do not learn from them.)

At birth, you began your journey of life-long learning. Throughout the process, you have made errors and had missteps along the way. Some have been minor, while, others have been more difficult. There is no need to be shameful. Everyone experiences varied degrees of blunders; some more than others. Try not to make the same mistake twice. If you do, start a new commitment. Whatever the case, identify the key factors and apply or eliminate them in future experiences—learn from your errors. Your mistakes should not define you. You should define mistakes.

Writing/Journal/Action/Discussion/Reflection Prompt:

What is one mistake that you have made from which you have learned an important life lesson? What is one mistake that you keep repeating? What are the key factors as to why you continue to make the same mistake? Identify two factors in your repeated error and resolve to eliminate them moving forward in life.

Day 196

"Life is a journey not a destination." – Souza

Sorry, there is no fortune cookie, road map, crystal ball, equation, or oracle that will determine the steps that you will take during your lifetime. If there was one, it would not provide all the experiences, positive or negative, that were intended for you to travel. Without question, you should recognize an objective, devise a plan, set a course of action, and take control of your own life. If you veer in one direction or take a path that you have traveled before, do not fret. Keep moving forward. Enjoy the view as well as the detours. With dedication and your internal compass, you will arrive at your designated location on-time.

Writing/Journal/Action/Discussion/Reflection Prompt:

Do you believe life is a journey or a destination? Provide support for your response.

Day 197

Walk in faith.

Step with the assuredness that what you are hoping for will come to pass. Trust that you are being led in the right direction. Believe that goodness is your guide.

Writing/Journal/Action/Discussion/Reflection Prompt:

Most often, do you walk in faith or fear? Why do you choose this approach more than the other?

Day 198

Goal getter!

You should live life with plans, aspirations, and hopes. The most authentic way to make something happen in in life is to envision it, prepare for it, and achieve it. More people than you expect live life vicariously because they forego all or at least one of the three steps noted in the previous sentence. Be an individual who sees it, drafts it, and completes it for themselves. You might not succeed the first, second, third, fourth, or so on time. Try again and possibly with revisions based on the previous attempt. There are two possible outcomes—success and or more preparedness for the next time.

Writing/Journal/Action/Discussion/Reflection Prompt:

Are you a goal getter or just a goal setter? Explain why?

Day 199

"Keep calm and carry on." – British Government (1939)

Life will present obstacles, unexpected occurrences, and even challenges. During those times, it is best to approach the situation with a leveled demeanor, optimism, and wisdom. Of course, you do not comprehend all aspects of the matter at the onset but that does not warrant a negative reaction or response. Remember, all situations improve over time; however, your initial and proceeding responses are vital for the improvement.

Writing/Journal/Action/Discussion/Reflection Prompt:

Describe a situation in which you remained calm. Describe a situation in which you reacted in a contrary manner. What was key to your differences in reaction? Try to apply the positive aspects in the next potentially non-calm situation.

Day 200

Joy is contagious!

Blessedness, happiness, and blissfulness are emotions that have a ripple effect. When expressed by you, these emotions transfer to another individual and so on. Your immediate environment needs displays of your joyfulness, so spread joy.

Writing/Journal/Action/Discussion/Reflection Prompt:

Think of a time when you witnessed the transference of joy within a certain setting. If you cannot think of an instance, create one.

Day 201

"Have a mind that is open to everything and attached to nothing." – Dr. Wayne Dyer

Open-mindedness is one of the avenues through which you can personally grow—spiritually, socially, emotionally, and intellectually. Possessing an open mind is like coming upon a portal by which pathways are present. Each pathway leads to a different and undetermined adventure that can only be experienced once you begin to take steps along the path. As you move forward, it is essential that you be open to different ideas, put all biases aside, and welcome new opportunities. You might be amazed at the transformations that occur within you by the end of your journey (life) because you were inclined to discovery.

Writing/Journal/Action/Discussion/Reflection Prompt:

What is something that you have not been willing to see from another perspective? Why are you unwilling? What do you believe is the harm that could result from viewing this perspective differently?

Day 202

"If it was easy, everyone would do it." – Tom Hanks in *A League of Their Own* (1992)

Has anyone ever minimized your accomplishment or estimated your deed with these three words, "That is easy"? These three words stand for a simple and common way of trivializing the completion of a task or the skill of someone (else). Just because you were able to begin and successfully execute something that others might or might not be able to do to the level or with the ease at which you appear to have done it does not mean that someone else could do it or in the same manner. Neither allow such individuals to play down your feat nor discourage them. If they have what it takes, simply, allow them to prove their skill.

Writing/Journal/Action/Discussion/Reflection Prompt:

Discuss a time when you were told, "That is easy." Did you view this as positive or negative and why?

Day 203

Life is my favorite adventure.

With the unexpected, unpredictable, and unprecedented moments, how could it not be?

Writing/Journal/Action/Discussion/Reflection Prompt:

Is life an adventure to you? In what ways is it or is it not for you?

Day 204

If you can't be kind… Be quiet.

Words have intent. Words are constructive and destructive. Your use of words has purpose. During times of doubt, say something that is positive and beneficial to others and/or about the situation. If the alternative is the only possibility, choose to let the silence speak for you.

Writing/Journal/Action/Discussion/Reflection Prompt:

Think about a time when you used words to build up someone. Think about a time when you used words to tear down someone. What was your ultimate intention during both times? How can you lessen the number of instances in which you aim to do harm with your words? Share your thoughts with another person.

Day 205

(Community = Common "unity," "common," "unit," "commun[e]." Room 207 is a "CommUNITY.") – For educators and students to apply

My classroom is a community. Every individual brings with them into the classroom unique: life perspective, experience, culture, religion, belief, hurt, joy, success, disappointment, bias, anger, hope, and much more. Each of these things brought as well as the individual have value. Rather than focus on the differences from a deficit point of view, focus on the difference from a celebratory vantage. Find ways to connect the individuals via the contrasts. By doing this, you begin to create unity. Dialogue is key. In dialogue, you engage in both speaking and listening, and you begin to commune with another. Through communing with others, you learn how much you have in common rather than what you have as differences. You see the differences as significant opportunities for authentic communion. In time, your classroom becomes a unit, a community (named only by the number outside the classroom door).

Writing/Journal/Action/Discussion/Reflection Prompt:

Can you think of a classroom that you have been in that felt like a community? Why did it? Can you think of a classroom that you have been in that did not feel like a community? Why did it not?

Day 206

Write your own story.

You are the author of your life. You are your own protagonist (or antagonist). Other people are secondary, whether major or minor or flat or round characters, in the telling of your narrative. Create your storyline/plot. Find your **exposition**. Make each step of the **rising action** deliberate as you reach the **climax**. With the forethought of possibility, do not allow the **falling action** to have the final word in your account because the **resolution** is yours for the taking and the writing of your story. Each day, put pen(cil) to paper/fingers to keys literally and figuratively.

Writing/Journal/Action/Discussion/Reflection Prompt:

From the bolded words in today's statement, select one word and draft that aspect of your present story/life. Moving forward, be mindful of and intentional about each aspect of your story/life's plot.

Day 207

"She believed she could, so she did. [He believed he could, so he did. They believed they could, so they did.]" – R. S. Grey

Your belief in yourself is vital to your sustainability and overall success. If no one else believes, that does not give you permission to doubt. Gender is not relevant with this statement. Defy the gender norms. Resist the doubters. Believe in yourself with every step that you take in life. You can and will, but you must never stop believing that fact.

Writing/Journal/Action/Discussion/Reflection Prompt:

What is something that you believe that you can achieve? How will you achieve it? Write six action steps towards making your hope your reality. Now, believe!

Day 208

Do it now.

Today is the best day to begin or finish something that you have put-off or put on hold. In life, there will always be distractions, obstacles, and new tasks to begin or complete that get in the way of something that is pending. When you set aside an undertaking, you are merely delaying the outcome, which could be positive or negative. Before making such a decision, weigh the reasons and the consequences. If the reasons and the consequences require immediate action, put into motion the necessary steps, and act now rather than later.

Writing/Journal/Action/Discussion/Reflection Prompt:

What is something that you need to do now? Name it and act. Return to this entry later, and write why or how your prompt rather than delayed response had a meaningful impact in someone else's or your life.

Day 209

(Life happens.)

Every 365 days a year, unless it is a leap year, which happens every seven years, life happens. Whether you consciously or unconsciously think about it, good and bad things, expected and unexpected occurrences, and imaginable and unimaginable phenomena manifest during one's lifetime. You (and everyone else) are neither exempt nor spared from such experiences even if you are a "good" person. Consequently, during these moments, do not count yourself as fortunate or unfortunate. Simply, acknowledge and face the point in time. The good things, expected occurrences, and imaginable phenomena will return because the bad things, unexpected occurrences, and unimaginable phenomena will not last forever.

Writing/Journal/Action/Discussion/Reflection Prompt:

How do you commonly respond to "life happenings" that are negative?" How could you alter your perception of/response to negative experiences in the future? Remember, your perception is a key factor in how you recover and move forward, presently and in the future.

Postscript

On average, primary and secondary schools are in session for 180 calendar days. As such, educators are given 180 opportunities to impact the lives of students. With this book as a tool (, which provides 29 additional [209 total] days/quotations), employ one quotable each day in your pedagogical practices, curriculum, and instruction. It is possible to use these words of wisdom and insight as writing assignments, thought provokers, discussion points, and in a number of ways. My fellow educators, I believe that your students will not only appreciate such opportunities but also will further develop into empathetic individuals who positively— live by and learn from—contribute to their immediate community and the larger society as a consequence of your willingness and care.

On a final note, I suggest that you use a journal or notebook to expound upon and capture your thoughts. "I write entirely to find out what I'm thinking, what I'm looking at, what I see, and what it means. What I want [and don't want] and what I fear [and don't fear]." – Joan Didion

About the Author

Dr. Larissa T. McCormick holds a Ph.D. in Education and is a caring and committed educator, author (*Portrait Narratives of Caring Teachers for African American High School Students* [doctoral dissertation]), and published poet and photographer, who currently works as a high school English teacher in an urban school district in Indiana. She also holds a Masters of Philosophy (M.Phil.) in Education, a Masters of Education (M.Ed.), and a Bachelor of Arts (B.A.) in English Literature and Secondary Education. Dr. McCormick has a diverse professional background as well as areas of expertise and research in qualitative and quantitative methodologies, including systems; culturally responsive pedagogies (CRP); diversity, equity, and inclusion; cultural awareness and competency; critical race theory (CRT); transformative learning; critical inquiry and pedagogy; curriculum, instruction, and assessment; Pre-K – 12; the ethics of care (Nel Noddings' theory of care); and social justice matters.

Dr. McCormick believes that her role as an educator is a religious vocation or calling orchestrated by God, and she focuses on the development and well-being—academic, social, emotional, and psychological—of the whole student. Throughout her years in the field of education, Dr. McCormick has had the privilege to work alongside, inspire, and mentor of more than one thousand youth and young adults and has witnessed the impact and value of positivity and encouragement in the life of these individuals. Dr. McCormick believes in the power of storytelling and reciprocity. As such, Dr. McCormick wrote this book to give students, educators, and anyone who chooses a favorable circumstance to foster personal growth, development, and love for all humanity.

Made in the USA
Columbia, SC
15 January 2024